Praise for **R**

"Robert Fitterman has to be one of the best, smartest, and most accomplished writers in the country. ROB THE PLAGIARIST is many notches above the intelligent thriller; this is pure genius."   —*The New York Times*

"A pulse-quickening, brain-teasing adventure."   —*People Magazine*

"ROBERT FITTERMAN is my new must-read. ROB THE PLAGIARIST is fascinating and absorbing—perfect for history buffs, puzzle lovers or anyone who appreciates a great, riveting story. I loved this book."
—*The New York Times*

"This masterpiece should be mandatory reading. Fitterman solidifies his reputation as one of the most skilled thriller writers on the planet with his best book yet, a compelling blend of history and page-turning suspense. Highly recommended."   —*Library Journal*

"Exceedingly clever. Both fascinating and fun...a considerable achievement."
—*The Washington Post*

"WOW... Blockbuster perfection. Not since the advent of Harry Potter has an author so flagrantly delighted in leading readers on a breathless chase and coaxing them through hoops."   —*The New York Times*

"A thundering, tantalizing, extremely smart fun ride. Fitterman doesn't slow down his tremendously powerful narrative engine despite transmitting several doctorates' worth of fascinating history and learned speculation, "rob the plagiarist" is brain candy of the highest quality—which is a reviewer's code meaning: *Put this on top of your pile."*   —*Chicago Tribune*

"Intrigue and menace mingle in one of the finest mysteries I've ever read. An amazing tale with enigma piled on secrets stacked on riddles."
—*New York Times*

"A dazzling performance by Fitterman... a delightful display of erudition."
—*Boston Globe*

"In ROB THE PLARIAGIST, Robert Fitterman has built a world that is rich in fascinating detail, and I could not get enough of it. Mr. Fitterman, I am your fan."   —*The New York Times*

Rob the Plagiarist

Others Writing By Robert Fitterman 2000-2008

Rob the Plagiarist

Others Writing By Robert Fitterman 2000-2008

ROOF BOOKS
NEW YORK

ISBN: 978-1-931824-33-0
Library of Congress Catalog Card Number: 2008944144

Cover by Jean Foos.

Acknowledgements
Versions of several of these texts appear in: *Traffic*, *slash ubu* (www.ubu.com),
Model Homes, *Jacket*, and *President's Choice*. "[R E A D I N G]" first appeared as
a chapbook by housepress; "The Sun Also Also Rises" and "My Sun Also Rises"
first appeared as a chapbook with No Press; "1-800-Flowers" first appeared as
a chapbook with porci con le ali; "LIT" first appeared in Tim Davis' photogra-
phy catalogue Illilluminations (Greenberg Van Doren Gallery). Further infor-
mation on each text is available in the "Notes."

This collection houses several of my texts that were written since 2000 and that
have appeared in literary journals and chapbooks. Taken together, the sum of
these pieces reflects my continued interest in a poetics of plagiarism. So, finally,
this house may be your house. Most of the writing here is part essay, part poet-
ry, part libretto, part conceptual writing, and nearly all borrowed.

 This book was made possible, in part, with public funds from the
New York State Council on the Arts, a state agency.
NYSCA

Roof Books are distributed by
Small Press Distribution
1341 Seventh Street
Berkeley, CA. 94710-1403
Phone orders: 800-869-7553
www.spdbooks.org

Roof Books are published by
Segue Foundation
300 Bowery
New York, NY 10012
seguefoundation.com

CONTENTS

1. Medium   9
   Why I Do What I Do Why He Does
      What He Does   10
   Identity Theft   12
   1-800-Flowers   22

2. Small   29
   Bisquick/Bismarck   30
   LIT   32
   National Laureate   39
   [R E A D I N G]   45

3. Large   52
   Hi, My Name Is   53
   A Hemingway Reader   68
      —The Sun Also Also Rises
      —My Sun Also Rises
   This Window Makes Me Feel   90

4. Notes   106

✳ "It's not where you take things from—
   it's where you take them to."
                    —*Jean Luc Godard*

1. MEDIUM

Robert Langdon awoke slowly.

A telephone was ringing in the darkness—a tinny, unfamiliar ring. He fumbled for the bedside lamp and turned it on. Squinting at his surroundings he saw a plush Renaissance bedroom with Louis XVI furniture, hand-frescoed walls, and a colossal mahogany four-poster bed.

Where the hell am I?

The jacquard bathrobe hanging on his bedpost bore the monogram:

HOTEL RITZ PARIS.

Slowly, the fog began to lift.

Langdon picked up the receiver. "Hello?"

"Monsieur Langdon?" a man's voice said. "I hope I have not awoken you?"

Dazed, Langdon looked at the bedside clock. It was 12:32 A.M. He had been asleep only an hour, but he felt like the dead.

"This is the concierge, monsieur. I apologize for this intrusion, but you have a visitor. He insists it is urgent."

Why I Do What I Do Why He Does What He Does

Most of my writing over the past decade has been composed with borrowed texts from the web, classical literature, mass media, etc. *Most of my writing recently can be found on idiotprogrammer weblog, which is a hodgepodge of things I've been reading/learning or having opinions about.* Initially, I was interested in appropriation as a way to destabilize language beyond the strategies that I already knew, such as disjunction and minimalism. *Initially I was embarrassed, but now I'm proud of them.* Later I discovered that these interests were validated by conversations in the other arts, especially in music and art, where appropriative practices offered the possibility of navigating or even participating in the network culture at large, as we had inherited it. *Later I discovered that President Roosevelt had the exact same TV in his house in Hyde Park.* By lifting a chunk of language and reframing it in another context, I found that something new and relevant was happening not only to my writing but also to my experience as a reader of both poetry and culture. *By simply taking a piece of paper and covering the right hand side of the paper, he can think about what the keywords, dates and questions are.*

Over the span of a decade, the interest in using appropriated texts has grown substantially among poets, so as to include a wider field of practitioners whose work might overlap conceptual writing, documentation, flarf, sampling, pirating, identity theft, and a host of other hybrid strategies. *Over the span of a decade, only twenty to thirty percent come to an end; 3) Among workers aged thirty and above, about forty percent are currently working.*

For me, using appropriation—either wholesale or in smaller sampled units (no hierarchy here)—intersects several current conversations about consumerism, art and technology, readership, etc. *Can someone label this sentence for me using Shirley Method? Peter rode his bike home.* By replacing or meshing "authentic" text with found text, I hope to highlight a parallel disparity between the object and the commodified object (Buchloh). *Significantly reduce eDiscovery processing costs by culling and reducing the amount of data collected prior to submission to costly processing.* This is, in part, why I do what I do—not to replicate or exploit the original, but to turn up the volume on its difference as we drag these materials into our own expressions and carve our paths through the informational morass. *This is, in part, because it is married to something more than just a scroll.*

The dialogue about how this path is paved is a rich one that offers a vital playing field for artists and thinkers alike, and my aim is to contribute works that further that dialogue. *I cannot 'know' what 'we' need without you joining in the dialogue about how you see the 'we' that 'we' are'.* As Jacques Rancière asserts: "We can no longer think of art as one independent sphere and politics as another, necessitating a privileged mediation between the two... Instead, an artistic intervention can be political by modifying the visible, the ways of perceiving it and expressing it, or experiencing it as tolerable or intolerable" (Art Forum, March 2007). *As Jacques Rancière has convincingly argued, art today no longer exists in the regime of representation in which works of art could be defined as such in relation to stable criteria.*

IDENTITY THEFT
a talk with additions by David Buuck

Introduction:

In early 21st century poetry, both here and abroad, the tendency toward the borrowed, the purloined, the sampled, the appropriated, the plundered, the plagiarized, has not only been substantiated by a late 20th century generation of loosely defined experimental writers, but it has been even more fully realized by a wave of younger poets and artists today who are at home with both the practice of appropriation and its cultural frame. Is this development a natural outgrowth from the largely language-based technological advances of our age? Is appropriation a way for poets to participate in network culture? Does this participation lead to taking some ownership of our culture, or even responsibility? Is this a way to articulate our role in cultural production? And what, then, happens to identity in this inventory of borrowed sources? Do the sources themselves define us? Does the composition of these choices define our aesthetic or craft? In sampling, does our original text take a regular seat on the bus next to found texts? Can we express subjectivity, even personal experience, without necessarily using our own personal experience? Are our identities so fused and overwhelmed by consumerism that these distinctions are rendered meaningless?

1. Whose Body / Shopping Is This?

As a replacement to the more authentic rock groups of the 1960s, the early 70s ushered in glam and death rock groups like Alice Cooper, T. Rex, David Bowie, and others who arrived in drag or glam costume with an easily accessible pop sound and a keen awareness of the music industry. For a 1970s splintered youth, especially in the suburbs, struggling to find footing and identity in a rapidly shifting consumer culture, these bands offered not just a new identity, but several new identities all at once. Given the deep-rooted and somewhat uniformed identity of the "hippie" culture, these new alternatives came fast and furious—the vacuum was carefully filled by marketing strategist who foresaw the benefits of emptying a singular identity and refilling it with multiple identities. As artist Mike Kelley writes: "Glam rock was a music that fully understood the commercial music world and accepted its arena of façade and emptiness, using the image of the drag queen as a sign of its status… David Bowie adopts personas, throws them away at whim, and constantly reinvents himself for the market. He mirrors our culture of planned obsolescence. For consumer culture, it has been suggested, the constantly changing, chameleon persona represents empowerment." A decade later, Madonna offers an even more obvious version of this obsolescence. The Glam rock sound and image amplified these new complexities in a few trademark identity blurs: boy-man, man-alien, boy-child, boy-girl. These 70s teens became comfortable with changing, chameleon personas, which continues today to be a boon for advertisers and marketers—a corporation could appeal to several identities within one consumer. It is in this moment, this environment, where the binary model of self-other breaks down, and where appropriated personas take hold. *Today I am FUBU; tomorrow I'm all about Burberry.*

By the mid 1970s, marketing strategists, corporate advertisers, mall designers, muzak programmers, etc., had become so astute in luring parts of our unconscious selves that a new id-driven variety of teen alienation surfaced (i.e. buying clothes for the many different "yous"). Where the super-ego (in this Freudian fable) once moderated the desires of the id, now the super-ego houses multiple identities with multiple drives of its own (again, good news for marketing). And to further assist in the obliteration of the super-ego's control, shopping malls—in but one example—stun-gun us with warmly disorienting muzak, artificial-natural lighting schemes and plant-life, confusing floor plans, illogical parking structures, piped-in aromas, waterfalls, etc. And in this dizzying state, we are ready to shop, to take on the new identities of surfers, mountain climbers, rugby players, rap stars, or French school children.

American teenagers of the 70s and 80s became comfortable with these multiple identities where the real comes in many shapes and sizes. In the preceding generation, young people sought alternatives to the values that they had inherited, but then one system of authentic values (truth, genius, good, evil, etc.) had replaced an older one. In the consumer culture of capitalism, the saturation of mass media culture and the relentless machine of corporate advertising had created the kind of cultural simulacra that changed the game. As marketers quickly discovered, if the new, young consumer did not know what he or she wanted (salad bars, food courts), the market strategist could continually create new possibilities, fantasies, even new values or simulated values, crafted in board rooms, that exist side-by-side with "real" values. (The popular rise of the personal credit card only deepened the grooves on this path.) As such, for writers and artists coming of age in the 70s and 80s, the notion of multiple identities and appropriated identities is a sort of native language, a natural outgrowth of the multiple personas that have been engineered and then targeted by market strategists.

(Buuck) In this feedback loop of manufactured wants and 'actual' desire, where any firm lines between base and superstructure are abolished, and critical/ironic 'distance' is increasingly how far you live from an IKEA. We are more and more involved in a process that we participate in with both criticality and complicity. I vote with my wallet. Consumer culture actually invites a form of participation that is not only economic and political, but aesthetic as well. We literally fashion our identities through our consumption practices. My fashion is my foreign policy. Wolfgang Fritz Haug has argued that the terrain of commodity aesthetics is a crucial battleground in consumer culture today, wherein the category of the aesthetic—from branding to marketing to use—increasingly becomes the site of value production. The mass-mediated is clearly a ripe terrain for oppositional poetics, where, in Peter Hitchcock's words, we might work towards "a new kind of answerability to the human costs of globalizing capitalist consumer desire," though hopefully without falling into either moral superiority or a reformist consumerism that equates political critique and opposition to PC consumption. As commodity culture becomes near-total, token refusals seem less interesting than the much more thorny relationships we each have with our own habits, desires, longings, and the structural regimes that delimit and inform them.

2. American Sincerity and Plasticity

The Baudrillardian embrace of the plastique of American ersatz is so complete that the ironic distance that was once common has shifted to a kind of blur in the sincerity-irony divide. The terms and sensibilities of inauthenticity, camp, kitsch, etc. that were once given only marginal territory so as not to disrupt "authentic" art and literature, have become recognized tendencies in all of the arts as a significant expression of American culture in the past several decades. The hierarchy of value in art between the genuine and the appropriated has been breaking down for decades. The blurred borders between authentic and ironic is already part of our cultural currency. For example, I really like Alice Cooper as a sentimental throwback, *and* as rock music, *and* I find it cheesy and silly, *and* interesting as a reference to a particular moment that is an important departure from a more "authentic" rock. There is both an embrace and a critical distance. These plasticities are most successful when the work is only partially absorbed. And it is at this intersection where there is, instead, a kind of weaving in and out of the absorbed.

3. Are we really just talking about collage?

It has been stated repeatedly among poets that there's nothing new about appropriated texts—we have examples in collage, found text, and imitation. One important distinction to note is that in the practice of using appropriated texts today, the materiality, the found sources, are fore-fronted often in large, unmodified chunks—a paragraph, a page, a whole book. These found materials take on new meanings and new social affronts in their new contexts. The strategy is to reframe works that already exist in new contexts to give them new meanings. This distinction is closer to the one between readymade and collage. Collage brings appropriated materials together, via the composition of the artist, to a singular expression. The plagiarist takes a source and reframes it in order to call attention to its new context, to cull meaning from this shift. Further, the plagiarist promotes the instability of language as it pours into these new contexts. These new situations instigate uncertainty, which, in turn, instigates new ways to potentially realize our place as text artists in a network culture.

As evidenced in both the arts and the sciences, we are in an age of the recombinant: recombinant bodies, gender, art, culture. In this era of information culture or network culture, many artists and writers have opted for working with the abundance of material already available rather than contributing more knowledge to the overcrowded landscape of originality.

4. Production, Access, Copy

Appropriation has historically stood in opposition to the privileging of any text because, for one, it foregrounds the act of reframing the text which, in turn, shifts the original meaning of the content therein, and, two, it de-mystifies the privileging of any texts by removing its contents from their spiritual, ideological, religious or scientific frames. The appropriator sees all objects as equal, as equally up for grabs. The appropriator is interested in borrowing the material that is already available—not as a null set in retaliation to invention, but as a new way of *participating in* invention. In the words of the Critical Art Ensemble:

> The plagiarist does not simply inject skepticism to help
> destroy totalitarian systems that stop invention; it partic-
> ipates in invention, and thereby is also productive. The
> genius of an inventor like Leonardo De Vinci lay in his
> ability to recombine the then separate systems of biology,
> mathematics, engineering, and art. He was not so much
> an originator as a synthesizer.

Today, speed of production and accessibility work in tandem to invite a less guarded expression for everyone; today it is difficult to control who is writing what and when. As readers, we are forced to re-evaluate our judgments as to what is good or acceptable. Whatever power structure is in place for defining such values for us, finds itself on shaky ground when everyone is using everything available. Whoever makes a book of poems, an essay, a drawing, a photo, etc. can post it on the web immediately and have it viewed by hundreds or even thousands of readers. We can cut n' paste found images or video clips or parts of other texts to go with our online books. Who is monitoring?

What, then, is the value, historically, of original, unique art works? In *Ways of Seeing*, John Berger writes convincingly about commodification as the primary drive behind originality. After the invention of photography and the ability to reproduce images, the need (by art business-people, curators, academics, etc.) to promote original art is obvious— money. It's more difficult to create mystique around the copy. The worthlessness of the product in copied art flies in the face of the precious and valuable original art whose mystification, by market-driven necessity, has limited its accessibility.

Imagine a distilled moment where the whole of American culture—its images, ideas, language, etc.—is electronically laid out before us for our inspection, digestion, processing, and all of us will have access to it, and that day has arrived. It seems to me that for poets, this is an especially significant moment. Poets now have access to the language of countless individuals' feelings and ideas from any historical moment. It could be similar to how Pop Art artists benefited from the new vocabulary of images offered by television around 1960. In light of this access, the poet as shaman, as the singular keeper and sharer of personal experiences, as the <u>designated medium</u> to receive messages from the spirit, seems more restrictive than ever.

(Buuck) "Yeah but Rob, what about our 'heart and soul'? But Rob, do you think, not mentioning those issues, that Americans are not aware of them? But Rob, do you really imagine that there can be any political situation, let alone a crisis, that does not team with numerous contradictions and different class interests? But Rob, do you WANT to see Eddie naked? But ROB, do you want free phone service from your house, or what? But, Rob, what does that say about ebooks? But Rob, what the hell happened with you? But ROB, what about this scenario? But Rob, what about the DRAMA!?! But Rob, what everyone now wants to know is, can you stick that puppy on your Pentax?"

6. New Subjectivities

What happens to personal experience in all of this? I am interested in the inclusion of subjectivity and personal experience; I just prefer if it isn't my own. Today I have access to an unlimited number of personal utterances and expressions from the gut, or the heart. Why listen to my gut when I could listen to thousands of guts? And/or in another paradigm, my gut tells me what to include, perceive, conceive, etc.

In "This Window Makes Me Feel" (included in this book), I culled language from online searches of the phrase "this makes me feel" to compose, in part, a response to 9-11 without referencing the event itself. I was more interested in documenting the moment before the attack rather than after. And I was not surprised to discover that this collection of hundreds of voices expressing everyday general feelings was far more powerful and had far greater reach than I might have

achieved with my own singular "voice". Even though these respons-
es that I was working with were related to other contexts, either gen-
eral or specific, they became specific in this new context. This other
subjectivity is not meant to replace an authentic, or single-voiced
expression. Rather, again, I hope to illuminate the hierarchical rela-
tionship that many readers of poetry express; that somehow original
language expresses a deeper, truer experience. One of the foundations
reiterated in poetry workshops is that personal experience will bring
the poet to specificity, a voice, and that is good (for) poetry. The oppo-
site is also worth consideration: "If exchange is the criteria of general-
ity, theft and gift are those of repetition. To repeat is to behave in a cer-
tain manner, but in relation to something unique or singular which
has no equal or equivalent (Deleuze)."

*(Buuck) Kathy Acker created new identities—sexual and textual—through
theft and appropriation, reclaiming a feminist erotics from the patriarchal lit-
erary canon. Bob Perelman, in his poem "Autobiography," writes a self out
of pilfered texts; the "author" literally enacted by the old saw "you are what
you read." Dan Farrell, in "The Inkblot Record", alphabetizes thousands of
Rorschach test statements, into an uncanny portrait of both the bureaucrati-
zation of the self and the writer's drive towards description: "I see flags, two
flags, they are green and waving. I see some roots there. I see that all the time,
the shading and color. I see the eye. I see two dogs' heads there. I seem to asso-
ciate bats with some kind of terror. I slept by myself, I was afraid." Dodie
Bellamy's "Cunt-Ups" splices together her private erotic correspondence
with the diaries of Jeffrey Dahmer to reconfigure the narrative and genre
expectations of pornography and the confessional: "I consider myself to be an
atheist, I admit I pussy weep. Would you feel okay about states? I am cur-
rently on probation for thoughts mushy and oozing like runny yolks,
thoughts about age and ass." Writers such as Mark Nowak, Catalina
Cariaga, Kim Rosenfield, Rob Mannery, Yedda Morrison and several others
appropriate historical texts from the domains of popular culture, labor strug-
gles, advertising, ethnographic studies, etc., to interrogate the rhetorics of
such language use, as well as to make such histories live and breathe again.*

*History is an encyclopedia of the possible, in language as in life. Repetition stut-
ters alongside disposability, and new sublimes erupt in the resultant static. The
mall is the nature park, the horizon of the new pastoral. Poetics is the engaged
navigation of such conflicted terrains, and our choices are always political, even
as we might inhabit the attraction/repulsion nexus of that consumer culture.*

that increasingly seems to contain us in a near-complete totality of capitalist social relations.

"That last sentence cost me twenty bucks."

7. Q & A:

What Rob means is something like this: What exit do you live off?

I think what Rob means is that in the Nord Modular this 1/8 phase delay is done on purpose.

What Rob means is that you used to look like a corpse.

What Rob means is that if you can design all your Flash animating characters as a single Flash scene that can be played in one sprite channel, that is a good thing.

I think what's Rob means is have you ever sleep walked, or thought you have?

I think what Rob means is if you don't use the black and red color coded wire, your hair will start to fall out early and your sphincter might pucker, and it's possible your woofer cones will invert themselves spontaneously and begin producing reverse osmosis sound waves, which can really mess with your head.

I think what Rob means is "You should never ride over your head."

If what Rob means is that it's the only good song, well... EASY ACTION is very forgettable, especially for a band whose next album would be such a masterpiece.

What Rob means is that your mother had to go to the hospital because something has happened to your brother.

What David means is to extend the selection of the two rows that you have, over a bigger area.

What David means is that Jimmy wasn't a leader of very many men, and he does keep falling asleep a lot, and there are probably more leadership qualities in David's left sock.

What David means is that XSL is a template language and you have to learn to think in templates, not in for-each.

What David means is that the National Security Agency requires that he and I wear these dark glasses when we are out in public, so that we can protect our anonymity.

What David means is that it was outlined BEFORE it was written.

I think what David means is that the floating market design you have proposed fits under the 'so small an effect as to be not worth having in the game' category.

What David means is that disputes to be settled are coming to his door.

What David means is that we have experienced the same with same.

What David means is Lindsay Lohan is really good looking.

What does Rob mean by 'The user space will die very soon'?

What does Rob mean when he says they bring others with them?

What does Rob mean by "abusive churches"?

What does Rob mean when he talks about 'solids' in the must?

What does Rob mean in English?

What does "rob" mean?
What does David mean about "the customer isn't always right?"

What does David mean when he says, "You weren't as sick as your secrets. You were as sick as your truths"?

What does David mean when he calls him an organization man?

What does David mean when he says that he and Helen stood together "reinvented"?

What does David mean by the phrase "pluck my feet out of the net?"

What does David mean by this verse? Was his mother an evil person?

What does David mean by "searched me and known me"?

So what does David mean here when he says, 'I do not concern myself with great matters or things too wonderful for me'?

Also what does David mean by "POST"?

1-800-FLOWERS

Inventory As Poetry in Louis Zukofsky's 80 Flowers

1. ABOUT

Flowers As Verb To Begin

Zufosky's *80 Flowers* contains in
a folded greenhouse the poet's
catalogue of poetic strategies honed
finely finally late in life
after "A" after a lifetime
of experimentation begins this poetic
will as inventory of strategies
or index it is this

Methodology

that interests me most then
not the significance of each
reference overwrought and excessive but
how the catalogue of these
strategies in concert find use
found language appropriation transliteration condensed
lyric constraints all reverberating in
a richly acute acoustic attention

Constraints

Because this catalogue of strategies
drives *80 Flowers* my piece
1-800-Flowers is a critical discussion
sod in the same constrictive
verse 8-line 5-words-per-line structure updating
several of Zukofsky's sources 1-800
corporate histories how-to gardening relying
on Zukofsky's own books indexes

Sources seedlings

Goldenrod solid-day go ponder otter
may well lead to Hardy
Adams Chaucer Shakespeare Greek Latin
librettos Taylor's gardening encyclopedia Gray's
botanical manual advertising laborious scholarship
has hounded down each reference
probably to Zukofsky's glee given
the detail-trail his notebooks leave

Seedling Where To: A Close Reading

10-slender rods spring seed sway
the numbers *1* and *0*
as stem-and-bulb blows the letter
"s" from word to word
pollinating each word-front-back blowing "s"
off seed from seed*s* and
onto *sway* not *way* nor
away as slender rods sway

Seedlings sources

Thanks to Levi-Strauss's essay when
80 Flowers was sparsely journal
circulated Michele Leggott's booklength study
and others we find each
reference has been painstakingly illuminated
and this is part and
parcel of our larger engagement
with the poem but what

About Strategies

Bringing all of these tendencies
and shade tolerance to total

not spring snow mold yet
a culmination from Zukofsky's early
"Poem Beginning The" he writes
because I have had the
occasion to remember quote paraphrase
I dedicate this poem to

"Found Objects 1962-1926"

A near lifetime of them
where *personal prescriptions recede and*
one composes with what one
finds already there or so
Zukofsky recounts in this miniature
manifesto reflecting backwards an art
in found objects language predicting
the later *80 Flowers* dioramas

To What End

In his earlier poem "Mantis"
John Taggart observes how *armies*
of the poor's left unresolved
although Zukofsky's treatment of language
overall might infer a social
leaning *at least the implication*
that by virtue of his
treatment Zukofsky successfully objectifies his

Complex Emotion

toward the poor that is
to say if the poet's
compassionate emotion for the poor
cannot be finally determined it
nonetheless can be inferred from
his love of language his

consciousness of word combinations and
their constructions but can it

Pollen, i.e.

How then *does* this methodology
add up meaning the sum
of the montage of borrowed
texts in Benjamin's "Arcades Project"
does add up to a
response or document of a
social history Williams' "Paterson" composes
a somewhat similar social construct

In Arcades

Benjamin whims *earth copulating with*
itself engenders the cherry mobility
silently bunkered in these cloistered
streets as in an immense
and splendid monastery like refuge
every lawn gets winter kill
I'm an ex-chemical fertilizer junkie
Ask Fran any lawn tamed

Port Jefferson Mugables

Sometimes I feel like my
lawn is calling the shots
weeds we may not always
have emptied this meaning for
a top-growth peel-back of another
ye whaling in genteel anchor-tees
draped tweed overcoat lawn-chair
what ten meant to Tiziano

2. THROUGH

Another Index

Acts acts basic conciseness desire
economies form grammar history information
judgment knowledge length montage nature
object pleasure quantity reader satire
translation unity vital will affective
body construction duration editing fact
generalization humanity ineffable kindness literary
mass nonsense order perfections religions

Toll Free

There was the mechanicalism in
the high fog there was
the world autumn interest grows
now you can turn off
the sprinkler free lions in
the mist vacation a last
cigarette an instruction booklet the
acropolis after acreage in miniature

1-800-END/EDIT

Rains grammar private floral varieties
may vary check availability don't
let the sun go down
on me either wherever fresh
cut rose color can mean
true love no doubt purple's
liveliest most of all hues
it's all in the name—

Vanity Numbers

I dreamed I saw St.
Augustine Decline (SAD) arise, arise
as you are or aries
Kentucky blue flux ablaze flog
a new flushing meadow's no
private reality is and is
all in the station-to-station directory
Europe newsreels markets across being

Your Extension

You who were made for
this ringer change whatever makes
this whole *conventional poets have*
the idea that they're in
complete control name product industry
slogan benefit feature clever phrase
apes a pro rower bowler
every fourth beginning in the

The X in Content

Placed laces these next to
another laces places altogether tied
a life no less unless
as Aristotle says you bring
together unlikes enhanced service provider
consumers trust customers more when
accessible to whom do I
give my neat little volume

Nature Hearth

Scooped up adornment numbers boost
the structure accelerated bottom line

growth not high on mountain
climber's song list legit knowledge
style of leaves growing top-of-the-mind
awareness when they walk away
a day two days three
weeks later remembering your number

Utilization

Cattle eat fallen leaves outer
skin toy games jelly plum
porridges bark beehives bark humans
warps badly has a wide
range of uses light and
woolly wood properties a hound
when he cometh by the
roses consider for large-scale planting

2. SMALL

My father's family name being Pirrip, and my Christian name Philip, my infant tongue could make of both names nothing longer or more explicit than Pip. So, I called myself Pip, and came to be called Pip.

I give Pirrip as my father's family name, on the authority of his tombstone and my sister—Mrs. Joe Gargery, who married the blacksmith. As I never saw my father or my mother, and never saw any likeness of either of them (for their days were long before the days of photographs), my first fancies regarding what they were like, were unreasonably derived from their tombstones. The shape of the letters on my father's, gave me an odd idea that he was a square, stout, dark man, with curly black hair. From the character and turn of the inscription, "Also Georgiana Wife of the Above," I drew a childish conclusion that my mother was freckled and sickly. To five little stone lozenges, each about a foot and a half long, which were arranged in a neat row beside their grave, and were sacred to the memory of five little brothers of mine—who gave up trying to get a living, exceedingly early in that universal struggle—I am indebted for a belief I religiously entertained that they had all been born on their backs with their hands in their trousers-pockets, and had never taken them out in this state of existence.

BISQUICK/BISMARCK

Make any day Oktoberfest whether with this impressive stein on your shelf or in-hand. Cheers! The name, Betty Crocker, was first developed by the Washburn Crosby Company in 1921 as a way to give a personalized response to consumer product questions. Framed print depicting the battleship Bismarck following a mine clearance vessel during her first voyage. Company executives chose the name "Betty" because it seemed warm and friendly to them. Otto von Bismarck was born on 1 April 1815 at Schönhausen in Brandenburg, Prussia. The surname "Crocker" was borrowed from retired executive William Crocker. The story of the Bismarck is a unique one, which is full of heroism, power and elegancy. In 1949, actress Adelaide Hawley became Betty Crocker for many years. She appeared for several years on the Burns and Allen show, and even had her own TV show for a while. She also appeared in the CBS network's first color commercial, in which she baked a "mystery fruit cake". Battleship Bismarck had everything except good luck. Domestically, Bismarck extended the powers of the imperial government, adopted laissez-faire economic policies, fought the political power of the Roman Catholic Church in the Kulturkampf, and pioneered social welfare measures. Bisquick easy recipes use the ingredients you already have on hand to make a variety of delicious homemade meals. Bismarck sailed on her first and only mission, code-named Rheinübung, on 18 May 1941, accompanied by the heavy cruiser Prinz Eugen. By 1932, this scheme had become so popular that General Mills began to offer an entire set of flatware; the pattern was called "Friendship" (later renamed Medality). The Breakout of the Bismarck is one of the most famous events of World War II. According to General Mills, Bisquick was born when one of their sales executives met a train dining car chef who mixed lard and the dry ingredients for biscuits ahead of time. Heft a cold one in this 22 oz. ceramic stein with gold trim. A great "usable" alternative to the trophy. Bisquick is a staple in more than half of America's kitchens, and home cooks are hungry for ways to use it in everything from easy entrées to everyday baking. On 26th May, in a final attempt to slow her down, Swordfish from HMS Ark Royal took off to attack the Bismarck—this cover is signed by TWO of the aircrew from that attack. In Golden Valley, Minnesota, the Minneapolis suburb where General Mills is headquartered, there is a street called Betty Crocker. Heading north, then northwest, the German fleet made good and largely uneventful progress across the Norwegian Sea towards Greenland and the Denmark Strait between Iceland and Greenland, the gateway into the Atlantic. Today, original Bisquick is still the market leader, delivering its well-known pancakes and biscuits as well as delicious solutions to the daily dinner dilemma. Assemble the German Battleship Bismarck with this 1:700 Plastic Model Kit from the Dragon® Modern Sea Power Series. From 1930, General Mills issued softbound recipe books, including in 1933 Betty Crocker's 101 Delicious Bisquick Creations, As Made and Served by Well-Known Gracious Hostesses, Famous Chefs, Distinguished Epicures and Smart Luminaries of Movieland. This is the fascinating story of Otto Von Bismarck (1815-1898), a man who was driven and activated by pride, courage, and hatred to a destiny that changed the course of German history forever. A portrait of Betty Crocker first appeared in 1936, subtly changed over the years to accommodate General Mills' cultural perception of the American homemaker: knowledgeable, caring and Caucasian. The battleship Bismarck was named in honour of Otto Fürst von Bismarck, the architect of German unification and the arbiter of European politics during the second half of the 19th century. In 2005, the 10th edition of the Betty Crocker cookbook was published; a Spanish/English bilingual edition is also available that collects some of the more common recipes. As German chancellor, Bismarck directed his foreign policy at maintaining and strengthening the power of the German Empire. 1/570 Scale. Features 131 parts molded in light gray, full 2-piece hull with propellers and rudder, detailed superstructure with main armament, life rafts and boats, Arado float planes, cranes, masts, and range finders. Bisquick mix revolutionized baking when it was introduced in 1930. In 2001, the brand launched Bisquick Complete, a just-add-water biscuit mix that adds a warm, homemade touch to any meal. Bisquick Complete biscuit mix is now available in five flavors.

LIT

Each section   outlined below   is   an
independent   treatise   on   a
limited   aspect   of
            light   and   color :   we hope
     you enjoy your   **V**isit   and find

        the answers to your questions.   Old light   and
owl light. The light of a spotlight.
.   Constable thought that   "No two days
ar e   a l   ik e,
        nor even two hours; **neither** were there ever
        two l eaves of a tree   **alike since** the cre-
ationof the   w orld"   ,
     then in a   new way   he represented   light
in the open air,
                    the movement of clouds
across the sky.   Picture Lights

by Hogarth. Fine Art are the only   lights   available to
illuminate your   Fine Art exactly.
     Not to sound **overly**   **dramatic**, but
        the LED (light-emitting
diode) is on its way   an**d**   to outing
incandescent   fluorescent
bulbs.   You need the
            ElectroKraft **Lunar Module,**
which features   multiple photo-sensor light portholes
for   theremin-like
control.   He earned a reputation   during
the 1940s and 50s   as one of the…   crisp
shadows   and sculpted   beams

of　　　　　　　　light. A majority of th**e Com**mon natural
and artificial light

　　　sources　　　　　emit　　　a broad range of wavelengths that
cover   the entire　　　　　　visible light　　　spectrum, with some

　　　　　　　extending into the ultraviolet and infrared regions
as well.
In this section
　　　　　　　　　　　　　　　　　　　　　　we will
investigate　　some　　　of the basic
　　　theories　　　　　　　　about the nature of light.
Understanding　　how and where　　　a rainbow　ap**pears**

　　is
　　　　　　　　　　　　tied　　to　　　　　un　derst
anding　　　　　　　how　　　　　light
　　　travels.
As we know,　　　　life
　　　　　would be greatly　　・　hampered
　　without light.　　　　　　　We would　　　　bump
into things,　fall **off**　　**precipices** and　　　　live
our　　　lives

like albino　　　　　cave **salamanders.**

　　　　T h ey m ay n ot　　un d er s t a nd
　oth er　　　**p u l s a　t in g cod e s**

　　　　of s h i n e, but　th ey r ap　　f o r
e t e rn it y.
The reference materials listed　in this section are
an excellent　　source of　　　additional　　infor-
mation
on　the　diverse　　　topic of
　　　　anisotropic media.
　　　I saw shine　　forth　　　　　　a
mighty lite.

We are, in fact, seeing light—
light that somehow left objects
far **or near** and reached
our eyes. Light is all our eyes
can really see. Such human
fabrication must
seem like
Bruises of clustered lights.

Light has the quality
to reveal
it is opposite of dark or unknown.

The light **of a student lamp** sapphire light.

The red panel,
the third color of the spectrum, represents the
Light of Poetry. Included are refer-
ences to books, book chapters, and review articles,
which

discuss the theory and applications of the refrac-
tion and refractive index
and how they relate to the

physics of light and color. There are many
mil itar y and com me rc ial ap pli cat i o
n s that c an bene fit fro m fu rth er innov a tio n s in
the use of lig h t
for sen sing and im
a g ing.

The light and shad o w there de als wit h
buildings and rooms and objects (whereas in
Caravaggio, it's people .
To help with geometric understanding,
we will assume that light travels in rays. We
begin with
light rays moving through the air at
a constant speed and consider
the reflection of light. In 1657
the mathematician Pierre de Fermat postulated a simple prin-
ciple: Light bends or refracts
when it moves from one transparent
material to the next.

This is what causes prisms . We do lie beneath
the grass

In the moonlight, in the shade   of the yew-tree.
As light passes from one substance
                    into another, it will travel   straight
through   with no change.
              In the center   of   the   panel,
     Poetry is   mounted
       on Pegasus,   holding a   torch in
     one   hand   while reaching
toward   the light of
          the

     ideal.   First of all,   it's not very much
like emerald   light. Sam thought glass
fiber
          and light signals   might work.   If
the angle of the beam   is increased even further,   the light
will   refract with   increasing
     proportion   to the   entry angle.
His use of light still has an influence on modern cinema says director Martin
Scorsese.

To the intelligence   fastened by the senses you are lost   in
               a   world   of sunlight
                         where nothing   is amiss.   As   c it
i e s   flo od   them   selves
with ev er   more

          light,   scientists wo r ry
                    about   los ing   the nig ht
sky   and   irrevocab ly   dis rupti ng   noc turn al
rhythms.

     Look up   ,   earth child   ,   the
light is   all!

This card just happens to   have been   printed

a neutral gray color,

but more   importantly it   is a surface

which reflects exactly 18% of the light
which   strikes it.
Ten bright-red LED bulbs flash 120   times
per minute for up to 300 hours
and are   visible for more   than one-half mile.   Light
are the   spinning
favours, intangible tonight.
The Molecular Expressions Microscopy
Primer explores   many

of the aspects of visible light starting with   an
introduction to   electromagnetic   radiation
and con tinuing through to hu man   vision
and

the   perception   of c
olor.   Starting with Ole Roemer's 1676   break-
through endeavors,
the speed of   light has been
measured at least 163

times by more than 100   investigators   util izing   a
wide variety of different
techniques.   Many early photographers   were fascinated by
the idea of photographing   at night,   but in
the mid-nineteenth century the slow emulsions   in
use   and the lack of good sources of artificial
light   made this   more or less

impossible.
The   light of a magnesium   flare. The light of a
magnesium   flare.

Light are the spinning
favours, intangible tonight.

The magic of photography   lies   in the
light.   As an example,   a beam of light

striking water   vertically will not be refracted, but if
                              the beam enters

                    the water   at a   slight angle

it will be refracted   to a very small   degree.   Finally
in 1983,   more   than   300 years after   the first
serious

        measurement attempt, the   speed of light was
defined   as   being 299,792.458
                kilometers   per second   by   the
Seventeenth   General   Congress   on
Weights and   Measures.

          Light is a complex

                    phenomenon that is   classically
        explained   with a simple model   based on rays
and wavefronts.   But if your means are more
modest,   you can still build a light   tent   that gives you
better results

                         when   photographing
small   objects   up close.
                What is   extra light?
                              The light in the window
seemed   perpetual.

National Laureate

Alabama

Eagle and egret, woodcock and teal, all birds
gathering to affirm the last gasp of sunset.

Alaska

Maybe I should stay in bed
all day long and read a book
or listen to the news on the radio
but truthfully, I am not meant for that.

Arkansas

Then, as we talked, my personage subdued,
And I became, as Petit Jean, a ghost,

California

I can stand here all day and tell you how much
I honor, admire, how brave you are.

Connecticut

Dark grays and fainter
Grays of near fields and far hills
Motionless, his mind

Playing silently
Over and over with his
Worry beads of words.

Delaware

On her dresser is one of those old glass bottles
of Jergen's Lotion with the black label, a little round
bottle of Mum deodorant, a white plastic tray

with Avon necklaces and earrings, pennies, paper clips,
and a large black coat button. I appear to be very
interested in these objects.

Florida

We learn from our animals, if we're smart.
They know how to wait. They know how to run
To catch up. Much of their life is spent at windows.

Georgia

Loaded on beer and whiskey, we ride
to the dump in carloads
to turn our headlights across the wasted field,

Idaho

I imagined him wading the shallows of a mountain stream—
the breeze still cold off the higher snow fields,
the fish smell of fresh water, the pitched hum of insects
waking to the sun.

Illinois

Fact is, each breath becomes bone
becomes dust

Indiana

Hill Thoughts,
Midnight Flight

Iowa

The afternoons go by, one by one.
My old friend, who shone like a tropic sun
Amid the poets of our day, too soon
Grown wan and thin as the late May moon,

Kansas

In river country flint nodules rest
among limestone sea bottoms, unexplained,
glassy among the porous tangles of shells

Kentucky

I see her in a photograph I found,
unsmiling in a drop-waist dress. No telling
how the roaring twenties roared through here.

Louisiana

i search but i can not find out
the streets of my ancestors

nor any relative to receive me

Maine

When I was a child and angels argued slamming doors,
I lolled, feet up the couch, head on the floor

Maryland

Before I leave, almost without noticing,
before I cross the road and head toward
what I have intentionally postponed—

Mississippi

Behind the Ridge
The Seeking Spirit
Cry Life

Montana

Gray cloud like a sweater pulled over the heart of the moon.

Nebraska

Windmill. Stretch even the
Fingertips against sand-coated hills.
You can get there from here,
Sir.

Nevada

Treat your Mommy nice
and take her to Las Vegas—
she'll think you're swell.

New Hampshire

The city was brick and stone in the time
before glass and steel. In those days
the city was streets of women.

New York

Long ago you kissed the names of the nine Muses goodbye.

North Carolina

The only clouds
forming are crow clouds,

the only shade, oaks
bound together in a tangle of oak

North Dakota

Most poets are rooted in the natural world,
spokespersons for the inarticulate in nature.

Oklahoma

under her cool skin
the feet dipped in formaldehyde

to prevent sweating
a river runs.

Oregon

And you pretty much gotta trust Her,
even if that means twiddling your thumbs
while she makes Her way through Her medley–

Rhode Island

The dark barge works the length of braziers
humped like monks awaiting sacrifice;

South Carolina

Seeds of hope are waiting
in the sacred soil beneath our feet
and in the light and in the shadows,
spinning below the hemlocks.

Tennessee

For eighty some odd years
He rose with the rising sun
And many mornings got up at dark
For so much work was to be done.

Texas

Her skirt clings to her the way fog clings to a flower.
Her legs are curled up, her sleeping face soft like a saint.
Driving for hours a man thinks about how things are measured,
about how coffee always tastes better in small towns.

Utah

Neither of us can guess if they'll hurry
dusk along, those clouds that have loitered
all afternoon over the rooftops. From our window...

Vermont

When you come back to me
it will be crow time
and flycatcher time,
with rising spirals of gnats
between the apple trees.

Virginia

When the last cloud leaves
nothing behind—no
history, no trace of error, no
basilica to shelter a man—

Washington

oblivious to the fact
that anyone might be watching,
that he might be teaching us all
how to live

West Virginia

Then, that recognition would
reward me for all I'd undergone,
my bravery of thought, my refusal
of dishonest love, and my goodwill

Wisconsin

Although distance does not
matter, it's a long way
into the flat pine forest

Wyoming

The work of hunters is another thing:
I have come after them and made repair.

Note: Not every U.S. state has a designated poet laureate.

[READING]

March 13th: In conjunction with the exhibition Rosemarie Trockel: Metamorphoses and Mutations, Line Reading presents: Anselm Berrigan, Jean Day, Lyn Hejinian. Anselm Berrigan's books of poetry include *They Beat Me Over the Head with a Sack* (1998), *Integrity and Dramatic Life* (1999) and the forthcoming *Pictures for Private Devotion*, all from Edge Books in Washington. His poetry and reviews has appeared recently in *Crow*, *Pharos*, *The Poetry Project Newsletter* and *Shark*. Berrigan lives in New York City. Jean Day's books of poetry include *Linear C* (Tuumba, 1983), *A Young Recruit* (Roof, 1988), *The I and the You* (Potes and Poets, 1992) and *The Literal World* (Atelos, 1998). Her work has been in anthologies such as *In the American Tree* (National Poetry Foundation, 1986) and *From the Other Side of The Century* (Sun and Moon, 1994). Day lives in Berkeley. Lyn Hejinian's books include *Writing is an Aid to Memory* (The Figures, 1978), *My Life* (Burning Deck, 1980), *Oxota: A Short Russian Novel* (1991), *The Cell* (1992), and *The Cold of Poetry* (1994), all from Sun and Moon in Los Angeles. Her collaborations include *Individuals*, with Kit Robinson (Chax, 1988), *Sight*, with Leslie Scalapino (Edge, 1999) as well as *The Traveler and the Hill and the Hill*, (1998), and *The Lake* (2001), both with Emilie Clark and published by Granary Books. Hejinian's selected essays, *The Language of Inquiry*, was published in 2000 by the University of California Press. She lives in Berkeley. May 20th: Line Reading for Children presents Andy Rash. Andy Rash's first children's book, *The Robots are Coming* is forthcoming from Scholastic this spring. His cartoons have been published in such magazines and newspapers as *American Illustration*, *The New York Times*, *Raygun Magazine* and *The Wall Street Journal*. Rash will be reading from *The Robots are Coming*. May 22nd: In conjunction with the exhibition, "Between Street and Mirror: The Drawings of James Ensor," Line Reading presents: Kevin Davies, Renee Gladman, Lisa Robertson. Kevin Davies's books include *Pause Button* (Tsunami, 1992) and *Comp.* (Edge, 2000). His writing has appeared in such journals as *The Impercipient*, *Open Letter*, *Philly Talks* and *Raddle Moon*. A member of the Kootenay School of Writing in Vancouver, Davies now lives in New York and teaches at NYU. Renee Gladman is the author of two chapbooks, *Arlem* (Idiom, 1996) and *Not Right Now* (Second Story, 1998), and a collection of prose work, *Juice* (Kelsey St., 2000). Most recently, her work has appeared in *Conjunctions 35*, *Fourteen Hills*, and *Mungo vs. Ranger*. Gladman lives in Oakland, CA, where she edits the chapbook press, *Leroy*. Lisa Robertson's books include *The Apothecary* (Tsunami, 1991), *XEclogue* (Tsunami, 1993), *The Descent* (Meow, 1996) and *Debbie: An Epic* (New Star, 1997). Her writing has appeared in such journals as *Parataxis*, *Proliferation* and *Exact Change Yearbook*. She is a member of the Kootenay School of Writing in Vancouver, where she lives. Jackson Mac Low is author of over 25 books of poetry, including *Verdurous Sanguinaria* (Southern University, 1967), *Asymmetries 1-260* (Printed Editions, 1980), *From Pearl Harbor Day to FDR's Birthday* (Sun and Moon, 1982), *Twenties* (Roof, 1991), *Pieces o' Six* (Sun and Moon, 1992), and *Barnesbook* (Sun and Moon, 1996). His work has been anthologized widely. Also an artist and composer, Mac Low lives in New York City. Ange Mlinko is author of *Matinees* (Zoland, 1999). Her work has appeared in magazines including *The World*, *Lingo*, *The Hat* and *Combo*. Mlinko currently edits *The Poetry Project Newsletter* and lives in Brooklyn. APRIL 7: BRUCE ANDREWS AND JACQUES DEBROT. Bruce Andrews is the author of several landmark books of poetry including *I Don't Have Any Paper So Shut Up (Or, Social Romanticism)* and *Paradise & Method* (Northwestern University Press). Forthcoming is *Lip Service, the "Dante Paradiso dub,"* from Coach House Books, and the "Millennium Project," which will appear on the Eclipse website. Jacques Debrot is the author of *Confuzion Comix* (Second Story Books), and is the editor of the zine *9 to 0*. Known as one of the more challenging from-the-hip literary critics and provocateurs, he has published poems in *Combo* and at www.arras.net. APRIL 14: ROD SMITH AND REDELL OLSEN. Rod Smith is the author of *In Memory Of My Theories* (O Books), *The Boy Poems*, *Protective Immediacy*, and with Lisa Jarnot and Bill Luoma, *New Mannerist Tricycle*. *The Good House* and *The Given* are forthcoming in 2001. He edits *Aerial* magazine, publishes Edge Books, and manages Bridge Street Books in Washington, DC. Redell Olsen is the author of *Book of the Insect and Book of the Fur* (rem press). One of a growing crop of exciting younger writers coming out of London, England, she has an MA in fine art and has worked in video, performance, and installation. APRIL 21: SALLY SILVERS AND MAC WELLMAN. Sally Silvers is a NYC-based choreographer/performer whose theoretical writing, scores, and poetry have appeared in many journals including *The Drama Review* and *The Impercipient*. Her next dance performances are in NYC at Construction Company, May 5, 6, 7. Mac Wellman, one of the country's great innovative playwrights, has published several books including *A Shelf in Woop's Clothing* (poetry, Sun & Moon), *The Bad Infinity*, and *Crowtet I* (*A Murder of Crows & The Hyacinth Macaw*). He was co-editor of *From the Other Side of the Century II: A New American Drama 1960-1995* (Sun & Moon). APRIL 28: YEDDA MORRISON AND KIM ROSENFIELD. Yedda Morrison lives in San Francisco where she co-edits *Tripwire, a Journal of Experimental Poetics*. Her chapbooks include *The Marriage of the Well Built Head*, *Shed*, and *Apostasy*, forthcoming from Melodeon Poetry Systems. Recent work has appeared in *Primary Writing*, *Kenning* and *Syllogism*. Kim Rosenfield is the author of several chapbooks including *Rx, cool clean chemistry*, *A Self-Guided Walk*, and the book *Good Morning-Midnight-*. An Internet chapbook, *Verbali*, is forthcoming on www.arras.net. Since the fall of 1987, over one hundred poets have read in Dia's Readings in Contemporary Poetry series. These readings have included historic literary events, such as James Schuyler's first public reading. All events have been videotaped, resulting in an extensive archive of poets reading from wide spans in their careers. Thanks to a generous grant from the Lila Wallace-Reader's Digest Fund, selected audio from historic readings is being made available, starting with the 1987 season. Beginning with the December 9, 2000, reading by Jorie Graham and Charles Wright, recordings of entire readings will be posted. Readings are at 4:00 pm at 548 West 22nd Street and admission is $6, $3 for students, seniors and members. Readings will be introduced by the director of Dia's poetry program, Brighde Mullins. Readings in Contemporary Poetry is funded, in part, by generous grants from The Juliet Lea Hillman Simonds Foundation, Inc., Lannan Foundation, and Lila Acheson Wallace Theater Fund, with additional support from the Axe-Houghton Foundation. Saturday, November 18, 2000: Sharon Olds and Quincy Troupe. Saturday, December 9, 2000: Jorie Graham and Charles Wright. Saturday, January 13, 2001: John Ashbery and Robert Creeley. Saturday, March 31, 2001: Alan Dugan and Maria Ponsot. Saturday, April 28, 2001: Anne Carson and Bei Dao. Saturday, May 19, 2001: Ann Lauterbach and Alice Notley. MARCH Thursday, March 15th 8 pm, Reading at the Getty Center: Christopher Merrill & Tomaz Salamun. Co-sponsored with the Getty Research Institute. Admission is free. Reservations are recommended. The Getty Center, Museum Lecture Hall, 1200 Getty Center Drive, Los Angeles. Call (310) 669-2369 for more information or to make reservations. Thursday, March 29th 12:30 pm. Lecture on T.S. Eliot and

"The Waste Land" Tan Lin. Poet and professor Tan Lin will discuss "T.S. Eliot and the Use Value of the Obsolescent." Admission is free. 438 Clemens Hall, SUNY-Buffalo, North Campus, Buffalo. Call (212) 254-9628 for more information. Thursday, March 29th 7 pm. Poetry in Translation: Slovenian Poetry, Tomaz Salamun, Andrew Zawacki and Ales Debeljak. PSA's Poetry in Translation series continues with an exploration of contemporary Slovenian poetry. Co-sponsored with Housing Works Used Books and Café and the Slovenian Consulate. Admission is free. Housing Works Used Books and Café, 126 Crosby Street, New York. Call (212) 254-9628 for more information. Saturday, March 31st 6 pm, Poetry and Criticism: Poetry & Beauty Charles Altieri, Brenda Hillman, Reginald Shepherd and Cole Swenson. Introduced and moderated by Donald Revell. The third installment in PSA's Poetry and Criticism series explores the relationship between poetry and beauty, from the sublime to the subversive. Co-sponsored with Poets House. Admission is $8/ $4 for PSA Members. Wollman Auditorium, Cooper Union Engineering Building. 51 Astor Place, New York. Call (212) 254-9628 for more information. APRIL Wednesday, April 11th 8 pm, Tribute to Stanley Kunitz. Lucille Clifton, Mark Doty, Marie Howe, Galway Kinnell, Yusef Komunyakaa, Sharon Olds, Robert Pinsky, Gerald Stern and C.K. Williams. The New York literary community celebrates the career of Stanley Kunitz, the recently elected Poet Laureate of the United States. Co-sponsored with The Academy of American Poets, the National Writer's Voice and The New York Times. Ticket prices are as follows: Balcony seats $10/ Orchestra seats $15. Town Hall, 123 West 43rd Street, New York. Call (212) 274-0343, extension 18, for information about reservations. Thursday, April 19th 6 pm. NYC Poetry in Motion® Live: Hal Sirowitz & Nina Cassian. A reading to celebrate the continuation of the dynamic Poetry in Motion® program in New York City. A reception will follow. Co-sponsored with the New York Transit Museum. Admission is free. The New York Transit Museum is located in Brooklyn Heights at the corner of Boerum Place and Schermerhorn Street. Take subway lines 2/3/4 to Borough Hall; N/R to Court Street; A/C/F to Jay Street; A/C/G to Hoyt-Schermerhorn. Call (718) 243-8601 for more information or for directions. Friday, April 20th 7 pm. The 91st Annual PSA Awards Ceremony. The gala ceremony will feature the presentation of the 2001 Frost Medal to Sonia Sanchez by prize-winning author Chinua Achebe and the official announcement of the winners of the PSA Annual Awards. A reception, including a publishers' display of the latest publications from 30 journals and presses, will follow the ceremony. Co-sponsored with the New School. Admission is $10/ $5 for PSA Members. The New School, 66 West 12th Street, New York. Call (212) 254-9628 for more information. Tuesday, April 24th 6:30 pm. Poetry in Public Places: Poetry & The Natural World. Poetry in Public Places continues with an evening of landscape and language at The Field Museum, the renowned museum of natural history. W.S. Merwin will read from his work, with particular reference to his poetry on environmental subject matter. Co-sponsored with The Field Museum, The Guild Complex and The Poetry Center of Chicago. Admission is $15/ $12 Students/ $10 PSA Members*. *Discounts are also available to members of The Field Museum, The Guild Complex and The Poetry Center of Chicago. The Field Museum, 1400 S. Lake Shore Drive, Chicago. Call (312) 665-7518 for more information or for directions. Thursday, May 10th 8 pm: Reading at the Getty Center Marilyn Chin & Jeffrey McDaniel. Co-sponsored with the Getty Research Institute. Admission is free. Reservations are recommended. The Getty Center, Museum Lecture Hall, 1200 Getty Center Drive, Los Angeles. Call (310) 669-2369 for more information or (310) 440-7300 to make a reservation. APRIL 4, WEDNESDAY, 7:30, CAROLE SIMMONS OLES & MATTHEW McKAY. APRIL 11, WEDNESDAY, 7:30, KURT BROWN & to be announced. APRIL 15, SUNDAY, 7:30, JOANNA KLINK (poetry) & JOHN D'AGATA (lyric essays). APRIL 22, SUNDAY, 7:30, MAXINE HONG KINGSTON & FRED MARCHANT. APRIL 27, FRIDAY, 7:30, MICHAEL HELLER & CARL RAKOSI. APRIL 29, SUNDAY, 7:30, GLORIA FRYM & LEWIS WARSH. WRITERSCORPS READING: Judith Tannenbaum, author of *Disguised as a Poem, My Years Teaching at San Quentin*, and WritersCorps teacher, is joined in a reading by WritersCorps poet-coordinators and poet-teachers Janet Heller, Sarah Lenoue, Valerie Chow Bush, and Cathy Arellano. A very special evening with ERNESTO CARDENAL Thursday April 19, 7:30 pm, $5-10 donation. Special Location @ The Women's Building (3543 18th St, between Valencia & Guerrero) presented in collaboration with New College of California & Mission Cultural Center. World-renowned Nicaraguan poet-priest Ernesto Cardenal, former Minister of Culture under the Sandinista government, and among the most significant Latin American literary figures of the past half-century, visits San Francisco in a rare appearance, co-sponsored by The Poetry Center, New College of California, and Mission Cultural Center.

Among his many books to appear in Spanish and in English transla-
tion over the past decades are *Oracion por Marilyn Monroe y otros poe-
mas*, *Cosmic Canticle*, *Apocalypse and Other Poems*, *Flights of Victory*, and
Quetzalcoatl. Father Cardenal will read his poetry in Spanish, with
spoken English translations provided. Seating is limited! Ernesto
Cardenal was born in 1925 in Granada, Nicaragua. He attended the
University of Mexico (1944-48) and Columbia University (1948-49), as
well as the Trappist monastery in Kentucky directed by Thomas
Merton. In 1965 he was ordained as a Roman Catholic priest, and
developed a politics and practice he considers "Christian-Marxist."
He is well-known throughout Latin America and North America as a
spokesman for social justice and self-determination. Euro-San
Francisco Poetry Festival featuring poets: KATARINA FROSTENSON
(Sweden) TOR OBRESTAD (Norway) LUTZ SEILER (Germany) TAY-
LOR BRADY (San Francisco). Saturday April 28, 7:30 pm, $5 donation
@ The Unitarian Center, 1187 Franklin (at Geary). Join us for this
evening of readings by a unique international company of poets, with
appearances by Katarina Frostenson, visiting from Sweden, Tor
Obrestad from Norway, Lutz Seiler from former East Germany, and
Taylor Brady of San Francisco. The Poetry Center is co-presenting this
evening's event as part of the Euro-San Francisco Poetry Festival, run-
ning from Thursday April 26 thru Sunday April 29, featuring visiting
poets from throughout Europe alongside poets from San Francisco.
Check out the festival website at www.bigbridge.org for full details of
the weekend's events. The Poetry Center is located in Humanities 512
on the SW corner of the San Francisco State University Campus, 1600
Holloway Avenue 2 blocks west of 19th Avenue on Holloway, take
MUNI's M Line to SFSU from Daly City BART 28 MUNI bus or free
SFSU shuttle. The Unitarian Center is located at 1187 Franklin Street
at the corner of Geary on-street parking opens up at 7:00 pm from
downtown SF take the Geary bus to Franklin. The UC Berkeley Art
Museum is located at 2625 Durant Avenue in Berkeley, near Bowditch
parking in the pay-lot on Bancroft opposite the museum from
Downtown Berkeley BART walk 2 blocks south on Shattuck, 3 blocks
east on Bancroft or take the 51 bus to Durant & Bowditch. The
Women's Building is located at 3543 18th Street between Valencia &
Guerrero parking in the pay-lot at 16th below Valencia from 16th St
BART walk 1 block west, 2 blocks south on Valencia then west on 18th.
Readings that take place at The Poetry Center are free of charge.
Except as indicated, a $5 donation is requested for readings off-cam-

pus. SFSU students & Poetry Center members get in free. The Poetry Center's programs are supported by funding from Grants for the Arts-Hotel Tax Fund of the City of San Francisco, the California Arts Council, the National Endowment for the Arts, Poets & Writers, Inc., and The Fund for Poetry, as well as by the College of Humanities at San Francisco State University, and by donations from our members. Join us!

3. Large

Who made the world?
Who made the swan, and the black bear?
Who made the grasshopper?
This grasshopper, I mean—
the one who has flung herself out of the grass,
the one who is eating sugar out of my hand,
who is moving her jaws back and forth instead of up and down—
who is gazing around with her enormous and complicated eyes.
Now she lifts her pale forearms and thoroughly washes her face.
Now she snaps her wings open, and floats away.
I don't know exactly what a prayer is.
I do know how to pay attention, how to fall down
into the grass, how to kneel down in the grass,
how to be idle and blessed, how to stroll through the fields,
which is what I have been doing all day.
Tell me, what else should I have done?
Doesn't everything die at last, and too soon?
Tell me, what is it you plan to do
with your one wild and precious life?

HI, MY NAME IS   *a libretto in one act*

Two characters. Ben is lowered from the ceiling. On the other side of the stage, Rebecca is already in place. After a moment of being alone, various office "products" begin to be lowered from the ceiling and set in place in Ben's office cubicle. At the same time, the items that furnish Rebecca's space start to slowly ascend. Ben begins his monologue. "Parallel Text A," is spoken in a soft voice as a chorus. Simultaneously, at the other side of the stage, Rebecca recites her monologue, slightly softer than Ben's, and continues as a loop until Ben is finished. Similarly, Rebecca's, "Parallel Text B," is performed very softly, almost a whisper. Note: I encourage these directions to be ignored or modified by readers, directors or composers.

BEN: Hi, my name is Ben! I'm calling from PEOPLES WIRELESS. Is Rebecca Smith home? How you doing Rebecca? Are you satisfied with your cellular phone service? Not surprised... most people are not. Well, I have good news and it won't cost you anymore than your present provider even if you are under contract. Please, just hear me out. If you don't like what you hear, then hang-up and I promise no hard feelings... just joking. Because your contract with your present provider is nearly over, you have been selected by PEOPLES WIRE-LESS to receive a free FULLY-FEATURED cell phone by mail in a rebate program along with a special calling plan that includes FREE ROAMING, FREE LONG DISTANCE and many other up-to-the-minute features. Included with your new phone, PEOPLES WIRE-LESS also gives you value added services like CALLER ID, CALL WAITING, 3 WAY CONFERENCE CALLING AND VOICE MAIL etc. In addition, this package comes loaded with benefits for you. It's a limited promotion that is available through this special telephone offer for the low price of $35.99 monthly. Yes that includes everything. Prime time? Yes, that is unlimited during prime time. The rates are competitive—the same as you pay now, even less. What I want to do right now is go ahead and verify that I have your correct mailing address to start processing your order so that we can get this valuable package out to you. That's ok, you don't have to commit now—we'll send you the contract to look over and I'm sure you'll find it to your liking. Also, if you sign up within the next 10 days, you'll get the first month free. Yes. I guarantee it. I have your address as 1 Washington

Street Apartment 7A, NY NY 10013. Is that correct? GREAT! Well, this package brings along with it, a host of powerful features and value added benefits. BUT FIRST I do have a few quick survey questions, if you don't mind. You're so patient. Are you above 18 years of age? Correct? Which credit card currently serves you best (VISA/MASTER/ DISCOVER)? Why? This limited promotion is held every year for preferred customers of V/M/D, and you carry a debit or credit card with master/visa logo on it. Is that correct? As previously stated Ms. Smith, this special benefit package will be shipped to you by UPS within 3-7 business days. All you have to do is agree to a one-year plan at a low $35.99 per month. Included with this plan, you will receive unlimited minutes and 300 minutes primetime, for as long as you stay with us. And as a special offer we are also going to send you a free fully-featured cell phone of worth $250. AND I KNOW YOU WILL LOVE THIS PHONE? Why are you laughing? Really, it's a great phone, a great deal. I know you'll agree when you look over the contract. But first: I have some important information for you to write down. Do you have a pen and paper handy? My name is Ben Sietz—that's "S" like "Sam" I-E-T-Z and I am the cellular consultant issuing you your INITIATION package today. My representative ID is "A" like "apple" 4-3-9-2-1. Can you read that back to me? Great. You have a really nice voice, you know... Keep that pen and paper ready, because our verification department will be giving you the customer service number for your region. OK. What I need from you to get the ball rolling is: Please read me your name as it appears on your credit card. Don't worry, I'm not asking for the number until you agree to the contract, which I'm sure you will find satisfactory. Ok, Ms. Smith please keep all of that information available for verification. Please hold the line for a moment, while I transfer you to our customer care department so we can make sure your introductory package reaches the correct location. This might take a minute... (sigh)... (long pause)... I'm sorry that was pretty loud, eh? I'm here on the line while we wait, in case you have any questions... You've been really kind, and I have to say you have a really nice voice—did I say that before? I'm sorry, but I mean you sound really sympathetic, your voice does? I bet you're a really nice person... I'm sorry is that inappropriate? I don't mean to be inappropriate. Uh, I've just had a really bad day... a really bad few days... yeah uh-huh yeah. Well, I just went through a terrible break-up, but I'm sure you don't want to hear about that right? I mean... after all... right... thank you, you've been really kind... just hold the line and customer care should pick-up shortly... right... oh that... I mean, do you want to hear about it...? It's awful, you know... you're so kind... no, no, we were together for years, for like 3 years... she used to work here, we met here and then she quit and went back to school and I was, like, supporting her... you know what I mean? Yeah she moved in last year, we lived together and stuff... are you sure you want to hear all this? Are you in a relationship? No? Why not? I bet you're nice anyway? Anyway, I earned all the income. I don't know where to start... no, not really? Are you sure this is ok? Well, one thing is she started "going out with the girls" a lot more than she used to but I trusted her and said to have fun. You know what I mean? When she was out of town for a week with her folks I opened her cell phone bill and found call after call to the same number at all times of the day and night. She even called this number 5 minutes after midnight on New Year's Eve while we were at a party. I know, it's awful right... I'm not sure what's taking customer service so long... yeah, right... I know... I had no idea... I found the guy's house and sure enough there was her car in his drive way. I know, I know... you're right... neither she nor the chickenshit boyfriend would answer the door... yeah, right... is this ok? Have you ever had anyone cheat on you? Once she finally came home, she told she had a new boyfriend... that she had trouble telling me about, obviously, leaving me, all that... can you believe it... I know, right... OK, here's customer care... hello? Wait a minute... (*long pause*)... oops, I guess we lost them... let me try again... oh, well yeah... of course, I was angry but once I got over that I pleaded with her to hear me out. She locked herself inside the bathroom... what could I do? You know what I mean? I shouted what I had to say. I even blamed myself... am I keeping you from anything?... is this really stupid? It's embarrassing I guess... no? I mean I was apologizing for whatever I might've done wrong, however I might've contributed to our break-up. By that time I think my words started to sink in, you know what I mean? She came out of the bathroom at least. Was I wrong to apologize? I mean, I'm not perfect either you know? I told her I would beg and plead for her to get back with me... I just wanted us to be on good terms even if we were breaking up, I mean 3 years is a long time, right? What happened next? We talked a little and then she said she was moving out... yeah, just like that, within minutes... this was on Sunday... Sunday night... yeah... I know, it's awful... (*Hi, this is Jean from customer care...*) OK, customer care is finally on the line—you can go right through. OK. It was nice talking to you; thank you so much for your time.

REBECCA: No problem. Uh-huh. That's awful. When was this? Just like that? Um, then what? Right. Sure. Of course. Um, not at all. Uh-huh. Uh-huh. Sure. Not at all, uh, no. No, no problem. Uh-huh, I know what you mean. Uh-huh. Weren't you, uh, angry? OK. It's awful. I guess so. Um, I'm not sure—I think so. Yes, it's fine. Oh man. You shouldn't have, uh, done that. It is taking a long time. You didn't, like, have a clue? It's awful. You're kidding. Uh-huh. Yeah, I do. Uh-huh. Do you have friends you can talk to? It's OK, uh-huh. I guess. Uh, I don't know, it's complicated. No, not really. It's fine. Uh-huh. How long were you together? Uh-huh. Yeah, sure. So, like, what happened? OK. No problem, no problem. I don't know—it's OK. Uh-huh. I'm sorry to hear that. No, it's OK. (*Pause.*) Does it? Um, I think you did. It's OK. People tell me that. No problem. OK, I'm holding. Was that you? OK. All right. OK. That's REBECCA "T" like "Teresa" SMITH. Uh, I'm not, um, giving you my credit card number. OK. Thanks. Yeah, it's A-4-3-9-2-1. OK. OK, I got it. OK. I'll look it over. (*Laughs*). OK. Uh-huh. I see. All right. Yes, I do. Um, why do you want to know? Yes I am. Um, all right I guess. Yes, that's right. Is that for sure? OK. I'm not going to, um, commit to anything over the phone. OK. OK. Um, what about prime time? Does that, uh, include everything? I see. OK. OK. Hmmm. I'm not interested thanks. Not really. Um, OK. This is she. Hello.

PARALLEL TEXT A   (CHORUS)

Wide Office Cubicle Panel/Partition.

Easy ONE TOOL installation with Free Shipping. Product is compat-
ible with Herman Miller® Action Office. Please remember to order
your CONNECTORS and select your fabric and trim color choices
from our menu. Manufactured with acoustical batting. "Helps to con-
trol noise!" Note: Panels are not free standing. Wire management and
power sold separately. 34" High X 12" Wide Office Cubicle
Panel/Partition. HA3412. $149.00.

Contemporary Task Chair w/ Arm Rests.

Great value featuring extra wide 19"W x 17"D seat and 19"W x 21"H
back. Includes pneumatic gas lift for adjusting the seat height from
18"-21"H. Spring tilt tension adjusts the back recline and locks for-
ward to keep chair in an upright position. Large 10" x 3" armrests are
padded for extra comfort. Olefin blend fabric upholstery. Stylish
brush finished metal base with casters. Price: $62.00.

Partition Additions Cubicle Wall Spring Clips.

Holds 40 Sheets, Graphite, 4-Pack, $2.59/PK. Item No./AKA:
FEL75270. Symbols: (Key). Additional Information: Contemporary
style coupled with unique versatility makes this plastic panel acces-
sory professional looking and functional. Fastens securely to any
tackable partition to help customize and maximize your workspace.
Easily repositioned utilizing steel points. Display important notes,
memos, phone lists, reference materials, etc. Holds up to 40 sheets. 1-
7/8"x5/8"x1-7/8".

Double Sided Tape with Dispenser for Permanent Application.

1/2"x450" 3M. $2.49/RL. Item No./AKA: MMM137. Symbols: (Key).
Additional Information: Self-Sticking adhesive on both sides for join-
ing and mounting board or paper. Transparent use for mounting to
acetate or glass. Durable for permanent application.

Precision-Crafted Dial-A-Phrase Dater w/ 12 Phrase Options.
Corporate Express Brand. $6.32/EA. Item No./AKA: CEB99034.
Symbols: (Key). Additional Information: Dial-A-Phrase offers; Eleven
phrases plus date: Answered, Canceled, Billed, Delivered, Entered,
Paid, Received, Shipped, Completed, Void, Filed and Approved
options. CEB99032, CEB99526, CEB99527, CEB99528 offer Date capa-
bility, Rec'd, Ans'd, Ent'd, Paid, A.M. and P.M. Height of words as fol-
lows: #0; 3/32" or 2.5mm, #1; 1/8" or 3mm, #1-1/2; #2; 3/32" or 5mm.

Economy Concealed Rivet Round-Ring View Binder.
1" Capacity, Letter, White EXP/Corporate Express $1.35/EA. Item
No./AKA: EXP60011. Symbols: (Key). Additional Information: Clear
overlay, two interior pockets with concealed-rivet construction. Sheet
lifters included on the 3" size. 8-1/2"x11" sheet size.

Steel Wire Paper Clips.
#1 Size, 100/Box. Diversity Product Solutions $.03/BX. Item
No./AKA: DPS40020. Symbols: (Key). Additional Information: Each
clip is formed to exact specifications from the finest quality steel wire
and is produced from a heavier gauge steel than standard clips.

Preferred Stainless Steel Scissors, 8" Straight, Blue Handles.
Corporate Express Brand. $6.32/EA. Item No./AKA: CEB10648.
Symbols: (Key). Additional Information: Corrosion-Resistant stain-
less steel blades ground inside and out for easy cutting. Blades are
molded into blue handles for added strength and longevity.

Regeneration Recycled Plastic Stackable Desk Tray.
Side Load, Letter, Black Rubbermaid. $2.02/EA. Item No./AKA:
RUB46106. Symbols: (Key). Additional Information: Regeneration
desk accessories work as hard for the environment as they do for you.
Made of 25% post-consumer recycled plastic, the full line of
Regeneration products will keep you and our landfills clutter-free.
Stacks and nests easily for convenient desktop sorting and filing. 13-
1/4"x9"x2-7/8".

Magnifier Lamp Base for Model# 7121 Lamp.
Weighted, Black. Electrix. $45.81/EA. Item No./AKA: ELEB60BK.
Symbols: (Key). Additional Information: Manufacturer's five-year
warranty. Architect's Clamp-On Swing Arm - Spring-suspension, 45"
reach arm. Adjustable clamp base (optional weighted base sold sepa-
rately). Metal shade with internal reflector increases light output and
keeps shade cool. Accepts 100W bulb, GEL-41036 (not incl.). Ul and
CSA listed. Made in U.S.A. Weighted Base Only 9 lbs.

Reversible/Erasable Universal/Vacation Schedule Wall Planner.
Undated, 36"x24" At-A-Glance. $22.39/EA. Item No./AKA:
AAGPM25028. Symbols: (Key). Additional Information: Page size:
36"x24". Reversible: Side One: Undated universal schedule ruled
with 22 lines plus notes space; Side Two: Undated vacation schedule
with 12 months and space for 25 employees. New bolder and larger
print is easier to see and read. Bright white background allow for eas-
ier viewing and reading. Sanford wet-erase marker included.

High-Profile Backrest with Adjustable Strap.
13"x4"x12-5/8", $20.74/EA. Item No./AKA: FEL91926. Symbols:
(Key). Additional Information: Modifies chairs to provide firm,
responsive support. Backrest is designed for chairs with a straight
back that offer little or no built-in support. High-Density foam main-
tains the back's natural curve, promoting the recommended neutral
posture. Adjustable strap holds cushion in desired position. Soft,
brushed covering is removable and easy to clean.

Earthwrite Recycled Pencils.
#2HB Soft Lead, Yellow/Green Eraser. Papermate. $1.56/DZ. Item
No./AKA: PAP12242. Symbols: (Key). Additional Information:
Hexagonal barrel, yellow finish. Casing made of 50% post-consumer
content. PMA certified nontoxic.

Fast-Drying Multi-Use Correction Fluid.
Bond White, 20ML. Papermate. $.99/EAItem No./AKA:PAP56401.
Symbols: (Key). Additional Information: New foam applicator for

smooth coverage. Corrects typing, handwritten, fax and photocopy errors, leaving surface like new for retyping. Quick drying with excellent coverage.

Plastic Coat Rack with 7 Hooks.
26-1/2"x2-1/4"x5-1/4", Gray. Deflect-O. $26.73/EA. Item No./AKA:DEF36709. Symbols: (Key). Additional Information. Modular coat racks feature multiple hooks for maximum use in limited space. Back panel is gray with gray hooks for a clean look. Hooks are made of plastic for durability. Features exclusive hidden screw mount system.

Shelf, End Right.
24"x24"x65", Avant Honey. Global. $573.30/EItem No./ AKA: GLBA2465ESHR1. Symbols: (Key). Additional Information: Adaptabilities provides the ultimate in flexibility and modularity. Designed to give you the freedom to create almost any configuration imaginable. Adaptabilities feature a huge array of highly versatile component products which can be configured into multi-user workstations suitable for intensive task functions.

900 Series Every-Day Swivel Task Chair.
Adjustable Seat Height, Gray/Black. Hon. $161.10/EA. Item No./AKA: HON7901AB12T. Symbols: (Key). Additional Information: Thick, wide cushions with bolsters for extra support. Fully upholstered chair back. Moderate proportions for smaller work areas. Multi-Layer foam padding provides all-day comfort. Multiple comfort controls. Optional arm kit available.

Binder Portfolio with 1" Ring Binder.
14-1/4"x2"x11-1/2", Black Nappa Leather, Executive Impressions. EXI45680. $59.90/EA Item No./AKA: Symbols: (Key). Additional Information: Supple drum-dyed quality leather, adjustable shoulder straps and padded retractable handles, multifaceted interior with pad holder, 1" capacity removable ring binder, one file pocket, two utility pockets, business/credit card holders and ID pocket.

Pencil Cup.

Punched Steel and Wire, Black. Stock #: ELD FG9E8800BLA. PRICE $8.40. QUANTITY EA. Express your unique style and taste with this contemporary pencil cup. The Expressions Punched Metal and Wire family is a unique combination, constructed of punched steel panels and durable wire framing. WEIGHT: 0.63

Desktop Organizer.

Letter, 12-5/6"x10"x2-3/4, Oak. Artistic Products LLC. Stock #: AOP 700. PRICE $9.42. QUANTITY EA. Letter size; 12-5/6"x10"x2-3/4. These premium desk trays give a sleek new look to a traditional favorite. Each piece is constructed of fine woodgrained laminate over pre-consumer recycled wood frames. Available in walnut and oak finishes.

Laser Labels, Mailing.

1"x2-5/8", 3000 Ct, White. Avery Consumer Products. Stock #: AVE 05160. PRICE $20.99. QUANTITY BX Packaging: 3000 EA/BX. Brighter white labels for sharper print quality are perfect for creating professional-looking mailings, shipping, bar coding and organizing. Just click and create with Avery templates in more than 100 popular software programs. 8-1/2" x 11" sheets.

Economy Mouse Pad.

8-1/2"Wx9-1/2"D, Blue. Compucessory. Stock #: CCS 23605. PRICE $1.29. QUANTITY EA. Smooth cloth mouse pad provides excellent mouse tracking. Features a nonskid rubber base that grips and protects work surface.

Wristrest.

Non-Skid Base, 18-3/4"x4"x1/2", Gray. Compucessory. Stock #: CCS 23710. PRICE $3.99. QUANTITY EA. 18-3/4"x4"x1/2". These soft, padded wrist rests help to relieve stress and fatigue for those long hours at the keyboard.

3-1/2" PC Formatted Diskettes.

DS-HD, 1.44MB, 10/BX. Compucessory. Stock #: CCS 71010. PRICE $3.29. QUANTITY BX Packaging: 10 EA/BX. The 3 1/2" diskettes features 100 percent error-free certification to ensure reliability and quality performance. Convenient bulk package delivers high quality data storage at great low prices. IBM formatted to save time.

PARALLEL TEXT B   (CHORUS)

AGNE Footrest.
$19.99. Designer: T Christensen/K Legaard. Seat: Solid pine, Stain, Clear acrylic lacquer. Leg: Steel, Pigmented epoxy/polyester powder coating. Foot: Poly-propylene. Seat diameter: 11 3/4 ". Width: 13 ". Seat height: 24 3/4 ". Seat diameter: 30 cm. Width: 33 cm. Seat height: 63 cm.

Lotil Hand Cream.
$9.99. Called "The Miracle Worker", this Lotil hand cream imported from England is regarded by many as the finest on the market. The first application will soothe and protect rough, chapped or cracked hands. Continued use insures the condition doesn't return. 1 oz. tube.

Stacking Acrylic Shot Glasses.
$3.95, reg. $4.95. Casual cocktailing in fun orange acrylic. Durable, stacking shot glasses with sham bases add a splash of color to indoor and outdoor entertaining. Molded acrylic. Hand wash recommended. Stored in an acetate tube.

Logitech IO Digital Notebook.
The io Digital Notebook is an ideal match for the Logitech io or io2 Digital Writing Systems. This pack consists of three notebooks: charcoal, red, and silver each with 120 pages that allow for simultaneous use. Take notes, send emails and brainstorm more... Product Code: 5115. Price $6.95.

Burt's Bees Beeswax Lip Balm.
$2.95. Burt's most popular product, chocked full of pain relieving protective ingredients to help soothe cracked, chapped or burning lips. Available in the .3 oz, old-fashioned yellow tin or the newfangled 15 oz. plastic tube (with 50% post-industrial recycled plastic).

SAMTID Floor/reading lamp.

$29.99. Shade of unbreakable plastic; minimizes the risk of injury. Highly mobile arm, easy to adjust. Tested and approved by an independent test institute; guarantees high electrical safety. Standard bulb E26 Max 100W. Base weight: Concrete, Polyethylene Base plate/ Tube: Steel, Paint Shade: Polypropylene. Height: 60". Base diameter: 10". Shade diameter: 9". Cord length: 5 ' 10 ". Height: 152 cm. Base diameter: 25 cm. Shade diameter: 22 cm. Cord length: 1.8 m.

SVANSBO Coffee table.

$24. Designer: Ehlén Johansson. Main parts: Particleboard, Fiber-board, Ash veneer, Ash veneer, Stain, Clear acrylic lacquer. Filling material: Paper, Underframe: Steel. Length: 35 3/8 ". Width: 11 3/4". Height: 17 3/4". Length: 90 cm. Width: 30 cm. Height: 45 cm.

A Paper Life.

New Hardcover Issue. Subtitle: My Story. Author: Tatum O'Neal. Publisher: Harpercollins. Retail: $24.95 Part Number: 0060540974BT. Release: 10/01/2004.

Women's Rib-Knit Henleys.

Tiny Fit. Fitted through body. Shorter length. Layering piece sold separately. Simply nice! Soft, stretchy cotton has narrow rib for a stylish fit. Seven buttons span chest placket, with long sleeves and embroidered icon on chest. Cotton/spandex. Machine wash. Imported. #314260 Price: $14.50. Size: XXS – XXL. All prices in U.S. dollars.

iPod.

$299.00. 5.9 ounces, 2.4 x 4.1 x .63 inches. Includes Apple Earphones, AC Adapter, USB 2.0 cable.

Fiesta Hand Tufted Rug.

$600. Designer Emma Gardner. Exclusive to Design Within Reach. Certified and labeled by RUGMARK. Hand tufted, 100% pure New Zealand wool.

Get Behind Me Satan.
New Music CD. Artist: <u>The White Stripes</u>. Record Label: V2 Records (USA). Retail: $18.98. Part Number: 638812725622BT. Release: 06/07/2005.

Avante 2-Slice Toaster.
$49.99. Item #: AVAN2SLT WC. Extra wide angled slots for easier and safer bread handling. Self adjusting slots allow even the toasting of all kinds of breads. New bagel feature to toast bagel interior without burning the exterior. Reheat setting, unique 2-position bread lift for easy toast or bagel removal. Safe-to-touch exterior and cancel button allows toast cycle to stop anytime. Electronic browning control (6 positions).

Tom's of Maine Natural Anticavity Fluoride Toothpaste.
Sizes: 4 oz, 6 oz. WINTERMINT ONLY: 3.5 oz, 5.2 oz. Flavors: Cinnamint, Fennel, Gingermint Baking Soda, Peppermint Baking Soda, Spearmint, Wintermint. Made with effective ingredients, our toothpastes are flavored with natural oils for great taste. We include the active ingredient sodium monofluorophosphate, sourced from calcium fluoride to safely clean and help prevent cavities. And, as always, no artificial sweeteners (like saccharin), preservatives or dyes.

Degreaser Concentrate - All-Purpose Cleaner.
Concentrated to work hard: Dissolves grease in seconds— wherever grease build-up is a problem. $8.39.

Capri Pants.
Silk sash slides through slanted belt loops. Faux back hip pocket. Three button accent on side seam hem slits. Front zipper. Hook and eye waistband closure with inside button. Inseam varies with size (size 6 = 26"). Linen, rayon, and spandex blend. Dry clean only. Made in the U.S.A. SKU 86508 Style# 341661024831. $89.00.

Batik Circles Pillow.
Featuring an outstanding one-of-a-kind circle design, this eye-catching creation is certain to become a topic of conversation. Use it to add extra color and comfort to a room. Made of cotton and polyester. A Pier 1 exclusive. (18 x 18″).

WiseWays - Herbal Moth Bars.
3 oz. Household Products Mists of Pleasure Laundry Freshener is a fragrant blend of essential oils to soak in a cotton cloth to toss into your washer or dryer load. Adds a sweet, fresh smell to your clothes and laundry room. Replenish the fragrance of the cloth with 2 capfuls of the oil from the small blue bottle every time you wash or dry clothes. Herbal Moth Bars Natural moth deterrent is completely non-toxic and replaces smelly chemical moth balls. $13.50.

Swedish Eggwhite Facial Soap.
An eggwhite facial, originally prepared by Swedish women in their homes, has been a weekly tradition for generations to maintain pure, glowing skin. $9.00.

Million Dollar Baby.
New DVD Movie – Widescreen. Actors: Hilary Swank, Morgan Freeman, Clint Eastwood, Jay Baruchel, Christina Cox Directed by: Clint Eastwood Studio: Warner Home Video Retail: $29.95. Pre-Order Release: 07/12/200. Part Number: 012569593237IE.

Berkshire Toeless Hosiery.
Product Description: Sheer Panty Hose with Control Top Hose without Toes! Behold, an incredible new idea in pantyhose: Our innovative Hose without Toes. Hose without Toes is a must for that sexy, open toe sandal. Show off your leg's natural elegance with this ultra sheer hose and still wear that strappy sandal! So get a pedicure and get ready to achieve the newest and most glamorous look in hosiery! $6.95.

Charmin Mega Roll Toilet Paper.
Try our largest size—the Charmin® Mega Roll! With the Charmin Mega Roll, you'll change the roll a lot less often than you did with Charmin regular rolls. That's because it has the same number of sheets as four regular rolls combined—so it lasts longer. And with the Charmin Extender, the Mega Roll easily fits into most standard holders. $8.95.

A HEMINGWAY READER:
The Sun Also Also Rises & My Sun Also Rises

> To look and to listen requires the work of attention, selection, reappro-
> priation, a way of making one's own film, one's own text, one's own
> installation out of what the artist has presented.
>
> —Jacques Rancière

THE SUN ALSO ALSO RISES

Book I

CHAPTER I

I am very much impressed by that. I never met any one of his class who remembered him. I mistrust all frank and simple people. I always had a suspicion. I finally had somebody verify the story. I was his tennis friend. I do not believe that. I first became aware of his lady's attitude toward him one night after the three of us had dined together. I suggested we fly to Strasbourg. I thought it was accidental. I was kicked again under the table. I was not kicked again. I said good-night and went out. I watched him walk back to the café. I rather liked him.

CHAPTER II

I am sure he had never been in love in his life. I did not realize the extent to which it set him off until one day he came into my office. I never wanted to go. I had a boat train to catch. I like this town. I can't stand it to think my life is going so fast and I'm not really living it. I'm not interested. I'm sick of Paris. I walked alone all one night and nothing happened. I was sorry for him but it was not a thing you could do anything about. I sorted out the carbons, stamped on a by-line, put the stuff in a couple of big manila envelopes and rang for a boy to take them to the Gare St. Lazare. I went into the other room. I wanted to lock the office and shove off. I put my hand on his shoulder. I can't do it. I didn't sleep all last night. I could picture it. I have a rotten habit of picturing the bedroom scenes of my friends.

CHAPTER III

I sat at a table on the terrace of the Napolitain. I watched a good-looking girl walk past the table and watched her go up the street and lost sight of her. I caught her eye. I saw why she made a point of not laughing. I paid for the saucers. I hailed a horse-cab. I put my arm around her. I put her hand away. I called to the cocher to stop. I had picked her up because of a vague sentimental idea that it would be nice to eat with some one. I had forgotten how dull it could be. I got hurt in the war. I was bored enough. I went back to the small room. I went over to the bar. I drank a beer. I could see their hands and newly washed, wavy hair in the light from the door. I was very angry. I know they are supposed to be amusing. I walked down the street and had a beer at the bar. I knew then that they would all dance with her. I sat down at a table. I asked him to have a drink. I was a little drunk. I got up and walked over to the dancing-floor. I took my coat off a hanger on the wall and out it on. I stopped at the bar and asked them for an envelope. I took a fifty-franc note from my pocket.

CHAPTER IV

I saw her face in the lights from the open shops. I saw her face clearly. I kissed her. I was pretty well through with the subject. I went out onto the sidewalk. I did not see who it was. I wanted to get home. I stopped and read the inscription. I knocked on the door and she gave me my mail. I wished her good night and went upstairs. I looked at them under the gaslight. I got out my check-book. I felt sure I could remember anybody. I lit the lamp beside the bed. I sat with the windows open and undressed by the bed. I looked at myself in the mirror of the big armoire beside the bed. I put on my pajamas and got into bed. I had the two bull-fight papers, and I took their wrappers off. I read it all the way through. I blew out the lamp. I wonder what became of the others. I was all bandaged up. I never used to realize it. I lay awake thinking and my mind jumping around. I couldn't keep away from it. I started to cry. I woke up. I listened. I thought I recognized a voice. I put on a dressing-gown. I heard my name called down the stairs. I looked at the clock. I was getting brandy and soda and glasses. I went back upstairs. I took them both to the kitchen. I turned off the gas in the dining-room. I had felt like crying. I thought of her walking up the street. I felt like hell again.

CHAPTER V

I walked down the Boulevard. I read the papers with the coffee and then smoked a cigarette. I passed the man with the jumping frogs. I stepped aside. I read the French morning papers. I shared a taxi. I banged on the glass. I went to the office in the elevator. I was looking over my desk. I held him off. I left him to come to the office.

CHAPTER VI

I sat down and wrote some letters. I went down to the bar. I looked for her upstairs on my way out. I saw a string of barges being towed empty down the current. I suppose it is. I walked past the sad tables. I watched him crossing the street through the taxis. I never heard him make one remark. I do not believe he thought about his clothes much. I don't know how people could say such terrible things. I don't even feel an impulse to try to stop it. I stood against the bar looking out. I did not want anything to drink and went out through the side door. I looked back. I went down a side street. I got in and gave the driver the address to my flat.

CHAPTER VII

I went up to the flat. I put the mail on the table. I heard the door-bell pull. I put on a bathrobe and slippers. I filled the big earthenware jug with water. I dressed slowly. I felt tired and pretty rotten. I took up the brandy bottle. I went to the door. I found some ash-trays and spread them around. I looked at the count. I had that feeling of going through something that has already happened before. I had the feeling as in a nightmare of it all being something repeated, something I had been through and that now I must go through again. I took a note out of my pocket. I looked back and there were three girls at his table. I gave him twenty francs and he touched his cap. I went upstairs and went to bed.

BOOK II

CHAPTER VIII

I could reach him always, he wrote, through his bankers. I rather enjoyed not playing tennis. I went often to the races, dined with friends, and put in some extra time at the office getting things ahead so I could leave in it charge of my secretary. I should shove off to Spain the end of June. I got a wire. I heard his taxi stop and went to the window and called to him. I met him on the stairs, and took one of the bags. I saw the long zinc bar.

CHAPTER IX

I came down. I would leave for Paris on the 25th unless I wired him otherwise. I stopped in at the Select. I went over to the Dingo. I wrote out an itinerary. I asked the conductor for tickets for the first service. I described where we were.

CHAPTER X

I was not at all sure. I forget what. I did not want to leave the café. I saw a cockroach on the parquet floor that must have been at least three inches long. I pointed him out. I asked him if he ever fished. I offered the guard a cigarette. I was up in front with the driver and I turned around. I saw he was angry and wanted to smooth him down. I sat in front of the café and then went for a walk in the town. I kept on the shady side of the streets. I left him sitting among the archives that covered all the walls. I went out of the building. I thought the facade was ugly. I went inside. I knelt and started to pray and prayed for everyone I thought of. I was praying for myself. I was getting sleepy. I thought I would like to have some money, so I prayed that I would make a lot of money. I started wondering. I was kneeling with my forehead on the wood in front of me. I was such a rotten Catholic. I only wished I felt religious and maybe I would the next time. I was out in the hot sun. I crossed over beside some buildings. I said I would go with him. I felt lousy. I put it in my pocket. I was blind. I certainly did hate him. I put the telegram in my pocket. I turned in early. I was asleep when they came in. I bought three tickets for the bus. I was sitting over at the Iruña reading the papers. I knew. I laughed.

CHAPTER XI

I went back to the hotel to get a couple of bottles of wine to take with us. I spilled some of the wine and everybody laughed. I got down and went into the posada. I gave the woman fifty centimes to make a tip and she gave me back the copper piece, thinking I had misunderstood the price. I turned around to look at the country. I opened it and showed him. I went out to find the woman and ask her how much the room and board was. I sat at one of the tables and looked at the pictures on the wall. I looked at them all. I went out and told the woman what a rum punch was and how to make it. I went over to the cupboard and brought the rum bottle. I woke and heard the wind blowing.

CHAPTER XII

I went to the window and looked out. I waved at him. I unbolted the door and went out. I hunted around in the shed behind the inn and found a sort of mattock, and went down toward the stream to try to dig some worms for bait. I drove the mattock into the earth. I lifted the sod. I dug carefully. I filled two empty tobacco-tins. I asked her to get coffee for us, and that we wanted a lunch. I went on looking for the tackle and putting it all together in a tackle-bag. I started out the room with the tackle-bag, the nets, and the rod-case. I put my head in the door. I thumbed my nose. I went downstairs. I was reading a week-old Spanish paper. I carried the rod-case and the landing-nets slung over my back. I shouted. I lifted it. I put back the slab of wood, and hoped nobody would find the wine. I got my rod that was leaning against the tree. I sat on one of the squared timbers and watched the smooth apron of water before the river tumbled into the falls. I put on a good-sized sinker. I did not feel the first trout strike. I felt that I had one. I banged his head against the timber. I laid them out, side-by-side, all their heads pointing the same way, and looked at them. I slit them all and shucked out the insides. I took the trout ashore. I put it in the shade of the tree. I sat against the trunk. I put my worm-can in the shade. I was reading a wonderful story about a man who had been frozen in the Alps. I walked up the road and got out two bottles of wine. I walked back to the trees. I spread the lunch on a newspaper. I went to sleep, too. I was stiff from sleeping on the ground. I stretched and rubbed my eyes. I disjointed my rod. I put the reels in the tackle-bag. I carried the other. I looked around on the grass at the foot of the elm-trees.

CHAPTER XIII

I went down to breakfast. I stopped at the post. I saw a girl coming up the road from the centre of the town. I had aficion. I found him washing and changing in his room. I leaned way over the wall and tried to see into the cage. I saw a dark muzzle and the shadow of horns. I went upstairs. I stood beside him. I remember from the war. I lost the disgusted feeling and was happy.

CHAPTER XIV

I do not know what time I got to bed. I remember undressing, putting on a bathrobe, and standing out on the balcony. I knew I was quite drunk. I was reading a book. I read the same two pages several times. I had read it before. I was very drunk and I did not want to shut my eyes. I heard them laugh. I turned off the light and tried to go to sleep. I could shut my eyes without getting the wheeling sensation. I could not sleep. I figured that all out once. I never slept with the electric light off. I had not been thinking about her side of it. I had been getting something for nothing. I thought I had paid for everything. I paid my way into enough things that I liked, so that I had a good time. I did not care what it was all about. I wished he would not do it, though, because afterward it made me disgusted at myself. I didn't know anything about the Eskimo. I didn't know anything about the Cherokee, either. I liked them, though. I liked the way they talked. I turned on the light and read. I knew that now. I would remember it somewhere. I would always have it. I usually sat in the café and read the Madrid papers and then walked in the town or out into the country. I went to church a couple of times. I told her that not only was impossible but it was not as interesting as it sounded. I felt quite friendly.

CHAPTER XV

I walked down the hill from the cathedral and up the street to the café on the square. I saw the bright flash as it burst and another little cloud of smoke appeared. I put down money for the wine. I explained to them that I would be back. I went down the street. I walked as far as the church. I asked a man. I paid and went out. I was introduced to the people at the table. I unscrewed the nozzle of the big wine-bottle and handed it around. I took a drink. I could feel it warming. I remember resolving that I would stay up all night to watch the bulls go through the streets at six o'clock in the morning. I could not find the key. I had been sleeping heavily and I woke feeling I was too late. I went back in the room and got into bed. I had been standing on the stone balcony in bare feet. I went to sleep. I had taken six seats for all the fights. I gave the extra ticket to a waiter. I told her about watching the bull, not the horse. I had her watch how Romero took the bull away. I pointed out to her the tricks. I told her how since the death of Joselito all the bull-fighters had been developing a technic that simulated this appearance of danger.

CHAPTER XVI

I walked out beyond the town at look at the weather. I left the crowd in the café and went to the hotel to get shaved for dinner. I was shaving in my room when there was a knock on the door. I finished shaving and put my face down into the bowl. I went downstairs and out the door and took a walk around through the arcades around the square. I looked in at Iruña for the gang. I walked on around the square and back to the hotel. I was drinking red wine, and so far behind them that I felt a little uncomfortable about all this shoe-shining. I looked around the room. I nodded. I met the friend, a Madrid bull-fight critic. I told Romero how much I liked his work. I reached to our table for my wine bottle. I explained that bull-fight in Spanish was the lidia of a toro. I had seen him in the ring. I told him only three. I did not want to explain after I had made the mistake. I introduced them all around. I rushed it a little. I spread a newspaper on the stone. I looked across at the table. I stood up and we shook hands. I noticed his skin. I saw he was watching. I think he was sure. I tapped with my finger-tips on the table. I translated. I went out.

CHAPTER XVII

I swung at him and he ducked. I saw his face duck sideways in the light. I sat down on the pavement. I started to get on my feet. I went down backward under a table. I tried to get up. I did not have any legs. I found I was sitting on a chair. I walked away from the café. I looked back at them and at the empty tables. I had never seen the trees before. I had never seen the flagpoles before. I felt as I felt once coming home from an out-of-town football game. I was carrying a suitcase. I walked up the street from the station. I could hear my feet walking. I had been kicked in the head. I was carrying my suitcase. I went on up the stairs carrying my phantom suitcase. I walked down the hall. I knocked. I opened the door and went in. I stood by the door. I had come home. I did not say anything. I stood by the door. I did not care. I wanted a hot bath. I wanted a hot bath in deep water. I could not see his face very well. I could not find the bathroom. I found it. I turned on the taps and the water would not run. I sat down on the edge of the bath-tub. I got up. I found I had taken off my shoes. I hunted for them. I found my room and went inside and got undressed and got into bed. I woke with a headache and the noise of the bands going by in the street. I remembered I had promised. I dressed and went down-stairs and out into the cold early morning. I hurried across the street to the café. I drank the coffee and hurried with the other people toward the bull-ring. I was not groggy now. I heard the rocket and I knew I could not get into the ring in time. I shoved through the crowd to the fence. I was pushed close against the planks of the fence. I saw the bulls just coming out of the street into the long running pen. I could not see the man because the crowd was so thick around him. I left the fence and started back toward town. I went to the café to have a second coffee and some buttered toast. I put one hand on the small of my back and the other on my chest. I came in. I followed them up-stairs and went into my room. I took off my shoes and lay down on the bed. I did not feel sleepy. I felt it with my thumb and fingers. I pressed up the wire fastener and poured it for him.

CHAPTER XVIII

I looked and saw her coming through the crowd in the square. I stood in front of the door. I tried the knob and it opened. I looked through the glasses and saw the three matadors. I could not see his face clearly under the hat. I think he loved the bulls. I sat in the down-stairs dining-room and ate some hard-boiled eggs and drank several bottled of beer. I drank it without sugar in the dripping glass, and it was pleasantly bitter. I began to feel drunk but I did not feel any better. I poured the water directly into it and stirred it instead of letting it drip. I stirred the ice around with a spoon in the brownish, cloudy mixture. I set down the glass. I had not meant to drink it fast. I was very drunk. I was drunker than I ever remembered having been. I went up-stairs. I put my head in the room. I went in and sat down. I looked at some fixed point. I went out the door and into my room and lay on the bed. I sat up in bed and looked at the wall to make it stop. I pretended to be asleep. I got up and went to the balcony and looked out at the dancing in the square. I washed, brushed my hair. I looked strange to myself in the glass, and went down-stairs to the dining-room.

Book III

CHAPTER XIX

I woke about nine o'clock, had a bath, dressed, and went down-stairs. I sat in one of the wicker chairs and leaned back comfortably. I drank coffee. I watched him come walking across the square. I only took a couple of drinks. I went out on the first roll with four kings. I rolled for the next two rounds. I went as far as the inner gate to the tracks. I watched the train pull out. I went outside to the car. I asked the driver. I paid the driver and gave him a tip. I rubbed the rod-case through the dust. I watched it turn off to take the road to Spain. I went into the hotel and they gave me a room. I washed, changed my shirt, and went out into the town. I bought a copy of the *New York Herald* and sat in a café to read it. I wish I had gone up to Paris. I was through with fiestas for a while. I could get a good hotel room and read and swim. I could sit in the Marinas and listen. I asked the waiter. I went in and ate dinner. I drank a bottle of wine for company. I had coffee. I told him to take the flowers of the Pyrenees away. I had a second marc after the coffee. I overtipped him. I spent a little money and the waiter liked me. I would dine there again some time and he would be glad to see me. I was back in France. I tipped everyone a little too much at the hotel to make friends. I did not tip the porter more than I should because I did not think that I would ever see him again. I only wanted a few good French friends. I knew that if they remembered me their friendship would be loyal. I hated to leave France. I felt like a fool to be going back into Spain. I felt like a fool. I stood in line with my passport, opened my bags for the customs, bought a ticket, went through the gate, climbed onto the train, and after forty minutes and eight tunnels I was in San Sebastian. I went to a hotel in the town where I stopped before, and they gave me a room with a balcony. I unpacked my bags. I took a shower in the bathroom and went down to lunch. I was early. I set my watch again. I signed it and asked him for two telegraph forms. I calculated how many days I would be in San Sebastian. I went in and had lunch. I went up to my room, read a whole book, and went to sleep. I found my swimming suit. I went into a bathing-cabin, undressed, put on my suit, and walked across the smooth sand to the sea. I waded out. I dove, swam out under the water, and came to the surface with all the chill gone. I swam out to the raft. I lay on the raft in the sun. I tried several dives. I dove deep once. I swam with my eyes open. I came out of water beside the raft. I lay on the beach until I was dry. I walked around the harbour under the trees to the casino. I sat out on the terrace. I sat in front of the Marinas for a long time and read and watched the people. I walked around the harbour and out along the promenade. I could not make out whom they belonged to. I had coffee out on the terrasse. I would see him there some time. I certainly would. I would certainly try to. I would leave a call at the desk. I had coffee and the papers in bed. I undressed in one of the bath-cabins. I swam out. I turned and floated. I saw only the sky. I swam back to the surf. I turned and swam out to the raft. I swam slowly. I looked around at the bay. I thought I would like to swim across the bay. I sat in the sun. I stood up. I walked back to the hotel. I gathered them up in the reading-room. I poked my finger along under the fold. I tipped the concierge and read the message again. I opened it. I had expected something of the sort. I saw the concierge standing in the doorway. I took out my fountain-pen. I went in to lunch. I did not sleep much that night. I had breakfast in the dining-car. I saw the Escorial out the window. I saw Madrid come up over the plain. I took a taxi. I saw the sign. I could not make the elevator work. I walked up. I rang. I rang again. I was undecided. I was happy to hear it. I would welcome the upbringal of my bags. I followed the maid's back down a long, dark corridor. I opened the door. I went over to the bed and put my arms around her. I could feel she was thinking of something else. I thought she was looking for another cigarette. I saw she was crying. I could feel her crying. I put my arms around her. I could feel her crying. I held her close. I stroked her hair. I could feel her shaking. I poured a little in my glass. I drank my glass. I tipped him and told the driver where to drive. I settled back. I put my arm around her and she rested against me comfortably.

THE END

MY SUN ALSO RISES

Book I

CHAPTER I

I was really impressed by them. I never met any one on that scene who read poetry. I mistrust people who make that much money. I always have some suspicion. I finally asked someone to find out if it was true. I played pool with him. I don't believe it. I found out how his girlfriend really felt about him when the three of us were at The Odeon. I suggested we go to Atlantic City. I thought it was ironic. I was kicked under the table. I wasn't kicked under the table. I said goodnight and checked out. I saw him again at Café Orlin. I thought he was all right.

CHAPTER II

I'm sure he had never been in love in his life. I hadn't realized how pissed off he was until he came to the restaurant I was working at. I never wanted to leave. I had to get to the 6 train. I love downtown. I can't stand to think about how fast my life is going by here, and I'm in some sort of daze. I wasn't interested. I'm sick of Tribeca. I walked alone one night all the way to midtown and nothing happened. I felt sorry for him, but there was nothing I could do about it. I broke down the waiter's station, divided the tips, and put Jane's into an envelope because she had the early shift. I went into the bar area. I wanted to lock up and get out of there. I put my hand on his shoulder. I can't do that. I was doing some coke the night before and hadn't slept. I could picture it. I have a bad habit of picturing my friends fucking.

CHAPTER III

I sat in a booth at Mickey's bar. I watched a very cute woman walk past me to the pool table and then disappear into a small group at the sign-up board. I caught her eye. I could see that she was kind of laughing to herself. I paid for the beers. I hailed a taxi. I put my arm around her. I put her hand away. I told the cab to stop. I picked her up because I was heart-broken over someone else and I was trying, somehow, to get back at her. I had forgotten how dull sex could be. I got hurt in a bad break-up. I was plenty bored. I went into the back room. I went over to the bar. I drank a beer. I could see a group of arty types glistening in white t-shirts outside the entrance. I was really angry. I knew that they were supposed to be cool. I walked down the street and had a beer at Magoo's. I knew that they all wanted to sit next to her. I sat down at a table. I asked her to have a drink. I was way drunk. I got up and walked over to the pool table. I took my coat off a hook and put it on. I stopped at the bar and asked if they had any stamps. I dug around my pockets for 50 cents.

CHAPTER IV

I saw her face in the subway window reflection. I saw her features look distorted. I kissed her. I was pretty well finished with the subject. I went out onto the street. I didn't see who it was. I wanted to get home. I stopped and read a plaque. I unlocked the door and thumbed through the mail. I said goodnight and went upstairs. I looked at them under the streetlight. I looked over my checkbook. I felt confident that I remembered their names. I turned on the bedside light. I sat with the windows opened and then pulled down the covers. I looked at myself in the mirror above my dresser. I put on a t-shirt and went into bed. I had two poetry journals, and I took them out of their envelopes. I read them all the way through. I turned off the lamp. I was thinking about the people I had just met. I felt wounded by some things that got said. I never used to realize it. I lay awake thinking and my mind jumping around. I couldn't stop thinking about it. I started to get depressed. I woke up. I heard my name called. I looked at the clock. I got something to drink. I went upstairs. I took them both to the kitchen. I turned off the lights in the living room. I felt like laying down. I thought of her walking up the street. I felt like shit again.

CHAPTER V

I walked down Greenwich Street. I read *The Times* with my coffee and then smoked a cigarette. I passed a man selling mechanical jumping frogs. I stepped aside. I read the Sports section. I shared a taxi. I knocked over a glass. I went to the restaurant by cab. I was looking over my schedule. I held him off. I let him take my brunch shift.

CHAPTER VI

I sat down and wrote some letters. I went over to Prescott's. I looked up at her window on my way to the bar. I saw a string of barges being towed empty down the Hudson. I guess it is. I walked past the depressing booths at the bar. I watched him crossing the street in between the traffic. I never heard him say anything. I don't think he thought about his clothes much. I couldn't believe that people could say such stupid things. I didn't feel like trying to stop it. I leaned against the bar looking at the pool table. I didn't want anything to drink and slipped out through the side door. I looked back. I went down an alley. I got in and gave the driver my address.

CHAPTER VII

I went upstairs to the loft. I put the mail on the table. I heard the buzzer. I put on my pants and sneakers. I filled a large pasta bowl with water. I dressed slowly. I felt tired and pretty rotten. I got a bottle of beer. I went to the door. I found some ashtrays and spread them around. I had a moment of deja vu. I had that sinking feeling of it all being repeated, like I had been out drinking with these people before and I knew how it was all going to turn out. I took some notes out of my pocket. I looked back and there were three girls at his table. I gave him a twenty and he touched his forehead. I walked home and went to bed.

BOOK II

CHAPTER VIII

I could always reach him, he wrote, through the American Express office. I was happy to stop playing pool for a while. I went to the horse races a lot at Belmont, ate out with friends, and put in extra shifts at the restaurant, making some more cash for a trip I was planning. I was planning to go to Europe at the end of August. I got a phone call. I heard his taxi stop and went to the window and called down. I met him on the stairs, and took one of his bags. I went to Le Zinc.

CHAPTER IX

I came down. I was supposed to leave for Paris on the 25th unless I phoned to say otherwise. I stopped in at Mickey's. I went over to Puffy's. I wrote out an itinerary. I asked a travel agent for a euro-rail pass. I described what was happening.

CHAPTER X

I wasn't sure of anything. I forget what. I didn't want to leave the bar. I saw a cockroach on the linoleum floor that must have been at least three inches long. I pointed him out. I asked him if he played pool. I offered the driver a cigarette. I was sitting up front with the cab driver and I turned around. I saw he was pissed and I wanted to calm him down. I sat on a bench in front of the bar and then went for a walk uptown. I kept on the shady side of Broadway. I left him sitting in a pile of books at the Strand. I left the building. I thought the façade was ugly. I went inside. I sat down and starting to daydream. I dreamt about everyone I had met. I dreamt about myself. I was getting sleepy. I thought I would like to be in a relationship, so I dreamt about being in a relationship. I was bent over with my legs crossed. I was such a lousy poet. I only wanted to be more like a poet and maybe some day I would. I was out in the hot sun. I crossed 6th Avenue beside some tall buildings. I said I'd go with her. I felt awful. I put it in my jacket. I didn't see it. I did hate her. I put the message in my pocket. I went to bed early. I was asleep when they came in. I bought 3 tickets for the bus. I was sitting over at Magoo's reading the paper. I knew. I laughed.

CHAPTER XI

I went back to the pensione to get a couple of bottles of wine. I drank some cleaning fluid from a glass that I thought was wine and everyone laughed. I got up and went back to the pensione. I tried to give the concierge a tip, but she gave it back to me, thinking I had misunderstood the price. I turned around to look at the countryside. I opened it and showed it to him. I went out to find the concierge and ask how much the room was, breakfast included. I sat at a table and looked at the maps on the wall. I looked at them all. I went out and told the woman what a Manhattan was and how to make it. I went over to the cupboard and took out a bottle of whiskey. I woke up and heard the wind blowing.

CHAPTER XII

I went over to the window and looked out. I waved at him. I unbolted the door and went out. I hunted around in the shed behind the pensione and found a hammock, and went down to the creek to try to find a good place to put it up. I tied the hammock around two small trees. I climbed in carefully. I filled up two wine bottles. I asked her if we could get some coffee, and that we were looking for lunch. I went on swinging in the hammock. I headed out the door with my backpack. I avoided her gaze. I headed down-stairs. I was reading a week old *Herald Tribune*. I carried my backpack and my duffle bag with some wine bottles in it. I leaned my duffle bag against a tree. I sat on the ground and watched the smooth sheet of water tumble into the falls. I put in a good-sized bottle. I banged it against a wall, accidentally. I had to take out all of my clothes, laid everything out. I picked through the glass. I sat against the trunk. I put the broken bottle in the trash under a shade tree. I was reading a wonderful novel about a guy who was obsessed with female pubic hair. I walked up the road and picked up two bottles of wine. I walked back to the trees. I spread out the lunch on a newspaper. I went to sleep, too. I was stiff from sleeping on the ground. I stretched and rubbed my eyes. I pulled on my crotch. I put the book back in my bag. I carried the other. I looked around on the grass at the foot of the elm-trees.

CHAPTER XIII

I went out for some breakfast. I stopped at the post office. I saw a girl coming up the road from the center of town. I had an ear. I saw my favorite poet thumbing through his books and taking off his sweater. I saw his dark side as the crowd shuffled in. I took a seat in the front. I stood beside him. I lost the depressed feeling and was happy.

CHAPTER XIV

I don't know what time I got to bed. I remember taking off my clothes, putting on a t-shirt, and standing out on the fire escape. I knew I was really wasted. I was reading a book. I read the same two pages over and over. I had read this book before. I was so drunk I didn't want to close my eyes. I heard people laughing. I turned out my reading light and tried to go to sleep. I could shut my eyes without getting the spins. I couldn't sleep. I figured that all out once. I always slept with the lights off. I had been thinking about how she must've felt. I had been getting something for nothing. I thought I had been fair. I worked hard, so I figured I deserved to have a good time. I didn't care about doing my writing. I wish he wouldn't have slept with both of them, though, because it made me envious. I didn't know anything about the graphic designer. I didn't know anything about the film-maker, either. I liked them, though. I liked the way they talked. I turned on the light and read. I knew that now. I would remember it somewhere. I would always have that. I usually sat at the Canal Street Coffee Shop and read the newspaper and then walked back home or into the East Village. I went to the Ear Inn a couple of times. I told her that not only was it impossible but it wasn't as interesting as it sounded. I felt quite friendly.

CHAPTER XV

I walked down the street from the St. Mark's Poetry Project and then east to a bar on Tompkins Square. I saw the bright flash of a small Con Ed explosion and then a little cloud of smoke. I put some money up at the bar for a beer. I told them that I'd be right back. I went down the street. I went as far as St. Mark's Church. I asked someone. I paid and left. I was introduced to the people at the table. I picked by the wine bottle and poured a round. I took a drink. I could feel it warming. I remember resolving that I would stay up all night to go to the Fulton St. fish market at 6 o'clock in the morning. I couldn't find my keys. I had been sleeping heavily and I woke up feeling I was too late. I went back to my place and got into bed. I had been standing on the wobbly fire escape in bare feet. I went to sleep. I reserved six seats for the Belmont Stakes. I gave the extra seat to a co-worker. I told her about watching the odds, not the horse. I had her watch how Cordero made his move. I pointed out the tricks. I told her that since a jockey was recently trampled to death, that there were more objections and inquiries.

CHAPTER XVI

I walked out beyond West Street to look at the river. I left the crowd at the Ear Inn and went home to shave for dinner. I was shaving in the bathroom when there was a knock on the door. I finished shaving and splashed some water on my face. I went downstairs and out the door and tried to take a walk through Soho with all the tourists. I looked in at the Ear Inn for the gang. I walked around aimlessly and then back to the Ear. I was drinking a pint of beer, and I was so far behind everyone that I felt uncomfortable with all this ass-kissing. I looked around the room. I nodded. I met a friend who wrote art reviews. I told him how much I liked his work. I reached over someone for my pint at the bar. I explained that poetry in the mainstream was like Norman Rockwell in Art. I had read a few of his reviews. I told him only three. I didn't want to explain after he caught me in a lie. I introduced him around. I rushed it a little. I spread the *Poetry Project Newsletter* over some plates. I looked across the table. I stood up and we shook hands. I noticed his coat. I tapped my fingernails on the table. I translated. I went out.

CHAPTER XVII

I insulted him and he missed it. I saw him shy away. I sat down on the curb. I got up. I fell off my chair. I tried to get up. I couldn't feel my legs. I ended up sitting on a chair. I walked away from the bar. I looked back at them and the place was empty. I had never seen those trees before. I had never seen a flagpole there. I felt like I felt once coming home from a high school soccer game. I was carrying a shopping bag. I walked up the street from the A-train stop. I could hear my feet walking. I felt like I had been kicked in the head. I was carrying my shopping bag with nothing in it. I went on up the stairs carrying my phantom shopping bag. I walked down the hall. The door was shut and I knocked. I rang the buzzer and went in. I stood by the door. I was home. I didn't say anything. I stood by the door. I didn't care. I wanted a hot bath. I wanted a hot bath in deep water. I couldn't see his face very well. I couldn't find the bathroom. I found it. I turned on the faucet but there wasn't any water. I sat down on the edge of the tub. I got up. I found I had taken off my boots. I looked for them. I stumbled to my room and went inside and got undressed and got into bed. I woke up with a headache from the noise of the trucks rattling on the street. I remembered I had promised. I got dressed and went downstairs and out into the cold. I walked down the street to the Club Diner. I had a coffee and then hurried along with the other people to the fireworks. I was awake now. I heard the firecrackers and I knew I couldn't get to the parade on time. I shoved through the crowd to see. I was pushed into the entrance of Wong & Wong. I saw rolls of firecrackers being lowered into a burning bin. I couldn't see the costumes because the crowd was so thick. I left the street and started back uptown. I went back to Club Diner and had another coffee and a toasted poppy seed bagel with butter. I put one hand on the back of my neck and the other on my forehead. I came in. I followed my roommates upstairs and went into my room. I took off my boots and lay down on my bed. I didn't feel sleepy. I felt it in my thumb and fingers. I twisted off the top and poured it for him.

CHAPTER XVIII

I looked out the window and saw her coming through the crowd on the street. I stood inside the door. I tried the front door knob to make sure it was locked. I looked through the glass and saw three guys in dragon costumes. I couldn't see any faces. I think he loved Chinese New Year. I sat in the Club Diner and had a hamburger deluxe and drank a coke. I drank it without ice in a fountain glass, and it was pleasantly spicy. I began to feel awake but I didn't feel any better. I took some ice out of my water glass and stirred it in. I stirred the ice around with a spoon in the brownish, bubbly glass. I set the glass down. I hadn't meant to drink it so fast. I was very depressed. I was more depressed than I ever remember being. I went upstairs. I stuck my head in. I went in and sat down. I looked at some fixed point. I left the living room and went into my room and lay on my bed. I sat up in bed and looked at the wall and wanted everything to stop. I pretended to be asleep. I got up and went to the window and looked out at the festivities. I washed, brushed my hair. I looked strange to myself in the mirror, and went downstairs and into the street.

Book III

CHAPTER XIX

I woke up at 9 o'clock, took a shower, got dressed, and went downstairs. I sat in one of the plastic seats and leaned back comfortably. I drank a coffee to go. I watched him walking cross the platform. I took a couple of sips. I went out before the draw. I stayed out the next two hands. I went over to the inner gate to the tracks. I watched the train pull in. I went into the last car. I confirmed with the conductor. I showed the conductor my ticket and the coupon. I pulled on my crotch and readjusted in my seat. I watched the train surface in Brooklyn. I went into the first car and got my ticket punched. I washed up, changed into my swimming suit, and went onto the boardwalk. I found a copy of the *New York Post* and sat in the snack shop and read it. I wish I had gone to Peter's. I was through with parties for a while. I could have gotten a ride there. I could have been sitting by his parent's pool and chilling out. I asked the guy at the snack bar. I went over and ordered a hot dog. I told him to leave the chips off. I had another coffee. I over-tipped him. I spent a little money there and he liked me. I would be back later and he would be glad to see me. I was back on the beach. I tipped the guy at the umbrella rental because I thought I was supposed to. I didn't tip the shuttle bus driver earlier because it seemed inappropriate. I felt like I wanted to make friends there. I felt like these were interesting people in our group. I hated to leave the city. I felt like a fool for committing to go to Philadelphia. I felt like a fool. I thought about my trip to Europe, opening my bags for customs, taking trains through tunnels, and sleeping in hotels that had seen their day. I liked this group of foreigners at the beach, especially Aldo from Argentina. I unpacked my beach bag. I took out a book and an apple. I was early. I set my watch again. I wrote some notes in the form of a poem. I calculated how many days before I left for Philadelphia. I went into the water. I went back to my towel, read the rest of my book, and took a nap. I undid the knot in my swimming suit string. I took off my t-shirt, put away my sunglasses, and walked across the smooth sand to the ocean. I waded out. I dove in, swam out under the water, and came up with all the chill gone. I tried to body surf. I lay on my back in the sun. I tried several different strokes. I dove deep once. I swam with my eyes open. I came out of the water next to Aldo's inflatable raft. I lay on the beach until I was dry. I walked around the shore past a volleyball game. I sat in front of the waves for a long time and read and watched the people. I walked along the shoreline and then out along the boardwalk. I couldn't make out whom they belonged to. I had another coffee at the snack bar. I would see all of them in the future. I certainly would. I would certainly try to. I gave each of them my phone number. I told them to leave me a message. I had my coffee and lay down on the blanket. I thought about getting dressed in the men's room. I swam out. I turned and floated. I saw only the sky. I swam back to the shore. I turned and swam out to the raft. I swam slowly. I looked back at the shore. I thought I might try swimming back to the shore. I sat in the sun. I stood up. I walked back to the bus stop. I gathered them up at the snack bar. I ran my finger along the rail. I looked for the bus schedule and found an old scrap of paper in my notebook. I opened it. I had expected something of the sort. I saw the bus driver standing in the doorway. I took out my fountain-pen. I went onto the bus. I didn't sleep much that night. I had breakfast on the train. I saw the Turnpike out the window. I saw Philadelphia come up over the bridge. I took a taxi. I saw the sign. I couldn't make the elevator work. I walked up. I rang. I rang again. I was undecided. I was happy to hear it. I would welcome some help with my boxes. I followed the landlady down a long, dark hallway. I opened the door. I went over to the bed and put my arms around her. I could feel she was thinking about something else. I thought she was looking for a cigarette. I saw she was crying. I could feel her crying. I put my arms around her. I could feel her crying. I held her close. I stroked her hair. I could feel her shaking. I poured a little in my glass. I drank it. I told the driver the address. I settled back. I put my arm around her and she rested against me comfortably.

THE END

THIS WINDOW MAKES ME FEEL

8:35 A.M., September 11, 2001

This window makes me feel like I'm protected. This window makes me feel like people don't know much about recent history, at least as far as trivia goes. This window makes me feel like I count and I enjoy knowing my opinions are heard so that hopefully I can help change the future. This window makes me feel like it's better to hear that other people have gone through it—it's like a rainbow at the end of the storm. This window makes me feel like the year I spent campaigning was worth it. This window makes me feel really good and also makes me feel like it heightens the sex when it finally happens. The window makes me feel like I did when I went to a heavy-metal hair stylist who wore a swastika belt buckle and I didn't say anything. This window makes me feel like violence is around every corner. This window makes me feel like there is a part of the news story that I missed. This window makes me feel like I have a tangible, relevant role in some ongoing process. This window makes me feel like I've won a prize, like I got a part in a movie. This window makes me feel like I do when I hug my dog. This window makes me feel like a special person to have them take a personal interest in my life. This window makes me feel like I'm on the ship in Ben-Hur. This window makes me feel uncomfortable like when people judge other people's sexuality. This window makes me feel like I'm giving back something to the place that gives so much to me. This window makes me feel like I've always been somebody outside looking in. This window makes me feel more Jewish. This window makes me feel like people rely on me to get the job done. This window makes me feel like it's raining outside and I feel dizzy and I like it. This window makes me feel blessed that I will be living in America for another year. This window makes me feel weird like I know what happened on that visit couldn't happen and it makes me feel good to see how things have changed for the better. This window makes me feel rich as I engage in this non-essential and expensive habit. This window makes me feel good to know that my company cares enough about its employees to even consider going for a program like this. This window makes me feel good knowing that the little things that I do can make such a positive difference in others' lives. This window makes me feel like I really shouldn't take extensive lie-ins on Sundays, that I've wasted most of the day, which makes me feel like I'm cheating. This window makes me feel more mature like when I volunteered at the hospital. This window makes me feel good and lets me know that I'm a pretty good player. This window makes me feel like my disappointment is a rock in my chest—it makes me feel hard inside. This window makes me feel like I'm actually doing some good and besides I get to sneak in a lesson on life. This window makes me feel like I have knocked down some pretty thick walls for others. This window makes me feel like I have a front row seat at the world's most ancient and mysterious show, that I am witness to the dawn of time. This window makes me feel unwanted and ugly and sometimes it makes me feel dirty when we make love because I don't know what he's thinking about. This window makes me feel rich but what a contradiction because I loathe capitalist hullabaloo yet still crave Vegas. This window makes me feel closer to God by worshipping through song. This window makes me feel like I need to go behind his back when I want to spend money. This window makes me feel like a man and nothing else has ever made me feel like a man. This window makes me feel like he's perfect no matter how mad he makes me. This window makes me feel almost as good as diving does because I'm online about 10 hours a day—I have very, very few real life friends—I'm pathetic. This window makes me feel like stupidity comes from the inside. This window makes me feel like I did when I was walking down the street one day and I met a perfect stranger who said that he was on his way to becoming a Ranger. This window makes me feel like I hate doing anything alone—I can't go to a restaurant and drink a cup of coffee in a café alone, shop alone, etc. This window makes me feel like I'm sticking way out in front and people actually stare quite blatantly at my belly which makes me feel freakish and shy. This window makes me feel like I'm in a Jacuzzi. This window makes me feel really happy that you decided to call me yourself. This window makes me feel like I do on sunny days laying down in my bed and listening to soft music—like having a home of my own. This window makes me feel like a bag of sunflower seeds. This window makes me feel powerful the way poetry does, or the poster I saw in a store window. This window makes me feel like I enjoy napping on the sunny floor, pouncing on a toy and eating tasty treats—if I come to a website that makes me feel uncomfortable, I leave it right away. This window makes me feel like I'm underwater. This window makes me feel like I end up with nothing, but somehow it makes me feel better. This window makes me feel like I have the best of city lifestyle, with coffee shops and boutiques right outside my door. This window makes me feel like the sun is touching my skin and I close my eyes and get sleepy. This window makes me feel like the said medicine has kicked in a 'lil and I feel good enough to type without going off on feverish tangents. This window makes me feel like a fool because when he sings, my wife puts her arms around the radio. This window makes me feel like a mass of flesh cuddles and strokes me under my skin. This window makes me feel nostalgic for things I've never done. This window makes me feel more or less like I'm drifting in space, or actually like I'm racing with space. This window makes me feel like locking the door. This window makes me feel like I get my love of nature from my dad. This window makes me feel like I'm cheating because I've been intimate with an old boyfriend online. This window makes me feel like he's choosing to go on a date with her instead of just stopping her from hurting me. This window makes me feel like my current generation is too often described in ways to imply that we need to be fixed or corrected. This window makes me feel like an even bigger goober because I didn't get my license until I was 22. This window makes me feel like a loser and the fact that I don't drink coffee nor drive a stick only makes things worse. This window makes me feel like the craftsman I am whenever I wear it and people comment on it. This window makes me feel like she's lying when she says she's only reached it twice and we've been together for two years and she says only twice. This window makes me feel like I have a really extended family, both here and in Thailand, who cares for me. This window makes me feel like the most spoiled woman in America. This window makes me feel like some kind of second-class global citizen living in a second-rate country. This window makes me feel like I'm scouring shops in SoHo and Tribeca even though I live in a small, historical town, so access to these kinds of products is usually limited. This window makes me feel like I'm still in the loop. This window makes me feel like his parents don't trust our relationship because they made this condition that the house would be in his name only. This window makes me feel like shit, although that little fact continues to be oblivious to the people who should be seeing it very clearly. This window makes me feel like an idiot because I need my mother to think that I look like one, too. This window makes me feel like a huge geek largely because I was never a cartoon fan before. This window makes me feel like something must be wrong or that he isn't satisfied with me even though I used to think our sex life was great. This window makes me feel like a dancer even though I don't have a dancer's build. This window makes me feel like I am worth something because they respect my ideas and treat me just like one of them. This window makes me feel like the quintessential mod from *Quadrophenia*. This window makes me feel like I am looking out of a cell and wishing I could return to therapy. This window makes me feel like a genuine rebel as I listen to some punk rock anarchistic lament on my Walkman. This window makes me feel like an evil person, and it saddens me, but at the same time, we can't change what we feel. This window makes me feel like it's one step forward and two steps back, thereby severely limiting my business's net growth. This window makes me feel like I'm worth absolutely nothing as I wonder what else they've covered up. This window makes me feel like a curmudgeon, and, besides, it's hard to stay up late for the real craziness if you're not chemically altered. This window makes me feel like a card-carrying member of the Family of Man. This window makes me feel like I am losing my identity as a Southerner—all too often I find myself buying gas at BP and not Jake's. This window makes me feel like I'm rushing into an uncertain future when my girlfriend talks about getting married, and she talks about it such a lot. This window makes me feel like my trust was wasted on you—can you explain this to me? This window makes me feel like I have an inferiority complex, like I know people are definitely better than me at dancing, singing, and various other things. This window makes me feel like I have to spend more time checking grammar and spelling, and that I wish I had learned more about English in school. This window makes me feel sad for many reasons, but I don't want people to think I'm going to hell—that's between me and God. This window makes me feel outraged... after all, I don't need the credit card... my track record has proved that I'm a poor manager of credit, okay? This window makes me feel nervous because he has been on medication lately but he hasn't been getting any professional help. This window makes me feel like reflecting on the mountain bike community and the ripple effect... for me, I never had a problem with hunters or trappers. This window makes me feel like I'm having some strange mental problem. This window makes me feel like what a bubble we all live in and what is the world coming to. This window makes me feel like it might not even be legal for his employer to fire him, and it might even be a violation of the Americans with Disabilities Act. This window makes me feel like canceling the rest of my order due to the shabbiness of the whole situation, even though I have been an excellent customer in the past. This window makes me feel excluded and it's just wrong that it's being held in a private home and not everyone in the community is welcome. This window makes me feel like how many parents and teens see no connection between God's word preached on Sunday and the decisions they make during the week. This window makes me feel unclean; maybe I need a shower, which is a good idea. This window makes me feel homesick, if you can call it that, like a family picture on the beach and the kids are snorkeling. This window makes me feel like these people are too real to be actors. This window makes me feel like I wouldn't be caught dead wearing one of those things on my head. This window makes me feel like I am essentially shamanistic; for whatever reason the drug rejected me. This window makes me feel like just walking away because I didn't mean to make you blush. This window makes me feel like the room has an entirely different feel to it now and the mural makes it a fun place to work. This window makes me feel like the sound squirrels make when you chase them away from the bird feeder. This window makes me feel like I have impeccable taste in music. This window makes me feel like his version of multi-culturalism makes me want to gesture at the deluge outside. This window makes me feel like I'm looking at Bombay and I'm thinking of my friends and family. This window makes me feel like I'm in a time machine, way in the future. This window makes me feel like I can feel the mushrooms popping out of my pores. This window makes me feel like buying that new scarf was an extra little purchase just to make my day. This window makes me feel like nothing is mine—even the wristwatch I'm wearing was given to me. This window makes me feel like I'm sitting in the back seat of a nappy yellow Buick. This window makes me feel like I'm being tortured with the sun beating down on me. This window makes me feel like I'm coming home to a house of dirty dishes. This window makes me feel they are letting me into a family music gathering, very pleasant indeed! This window makes me feel like I am traveling to their country without taking an airplane. This window makes me feel like, hello, was the word DUMB tattooed on my forehead or not. This window makes me feel like I am looking or listening through a retro-filter, but I like its direct authenticity. This window makes me feel like I am nothing but an object, an anonymous female figure to view. This window makes me feel like maybe if I am wrong I'll still have an "in" with the Big Guy because apparently God has trouble seeing through charades. This window makes me feel like a slacker—good thing I'm okay with that. This window makes me feel like my job as a baker is half done. This window makes me feel like I'm back in my first year of college in the dorm: "OK, my name is so-and-so, I'm from here-and-there, my major is something-or-other." This window makes me feel like I should own by now because there's a lot of real-estate going around here recently. This window makes me feel like I'm sliding off the ends. This window makes me feel like tiny things are beautiful, that there's humor in the industrial world, and that you can go slightly psycho and that will be even truer. This window makes me feel like an old lady because, after all, I am only a creep in my imagination—in real life I am very nice and unthreatening. This window makes me feel like we should all take the time to stop and smell the flowers. This window makes me feel like I can visit my heritage without even being there. This window makes me feel like they were excited with this project for nine months, and now I can do anything. This window makes me feel like I did something right for once—listen, I know these people and they will tell you if it's good or bad. This window makes me feel like I'm hearing the names of these plants for the first time. This window makes me feel like a bad person because I do second level technical support for them when I know I could do more. This window makes me feel like you're trying to act like you had nothing to do with it. This window makes me feel like kicking some ass. This window makes me feel like a freak because I'm probably the only 30 year-old virgin in America who isn't a priest, monk, etc. This window makes me feel like a fossil because the field has changed enormously in these past decades. This window makes me feel like a stalker—I need to calm down—but maybe next semester we can get to know one another. This window makes me feel like they really care about my opinion and I'm treated like everyone else is treated. This window makes me feel like a self-centered freak. This window makes me feel like the country mouse when I look back at my hometown in Wichita. This window makes me feel like more of a part of a dream, and fulfilling what God has planned for us in the future. This window makes me feel like they're really listening to me, even when they do most of the talking, and it's a real turn-on. This window makes me feel like I'm handling items in microgravity without changing my orientation. This window makes me feel like I'm not free to say what I want to say. This window makes me feel like I live in the woods. This window makes me feel a bit shaken up—I sleep with the window open, even in winter, with a loaded rifle and a flashlight handy. This window makes me feel like saying, "please, girl, stick it out with me... I feel a change coming over me." This window makes me feel more cocky and powerful when I have a good breakfast—don't eat anything you can buy from a place with a drive-thru window. This window makes me feel like, I don't know, it just makes sense to me—it's just my perspective. This window makes me feel unhip, out-of-touch, old, and I don't care if they are the latest fashion or on whose runway they were first spotted. This window makes me feel like I wish I could get up on the roof of my apartment building, but there's a revolving restaurant up there so no way. This window makes me feel like he is explicating her position as a post-linguistic turned Kantian position. This window makes me feel like I don't know you people, why are you here? This window makes me feel guilty because we've had far too much rain this year, and farmers like my mother's brother are really suffering. This window makes me feel like all of my education is for nothing and I don't know when I will ever get the right job. This window makes me feel like I am special and loved—when we do nice things for each other we feel happier and want to be together more. This window makes me feel less like a customer and more like a part of the team without talking computereze and without being talked down to. This window makes me feel like the inside is already a man, and I need to make the outside so. This window makes me feel neglected because he says he doesn't believe he needs to participate in these manufactured holidays. This window makes me feel even more alone than before with so many people checking up on me lately. This window makes me feel like I'm in Disneyland—my checkbook is balanced, the porch is swept, the plants have been watered, and almost all of my clothes have been put away. This window makes me feel better because I know I covered my ass. This window makes me feel sad because it reveals how melancholically beautiful England is, suburbs and all. This window makes me feel like I'm looking at mountains even though there aren't any mountains for miles and miles. This window makes me feel like everyone around me is giving the two thumbs up sign. This window makes me feel like I must be so unimportant to him if he tells me he was busy all day and that he didn't even have the chance to call me until late at night. This window makes me feel very insecure about my manhood, what with the pink artwork and the fucking unicorn on the front. This window makes me feel like trash and like everyone thinks I'm trashy being big on top and having to look like this. This window makes me feel very optimistic about the future of Latino entertainment. This window makes me feel significant in the *big man* circles, but I've learned that I am just a presentable prop for pompous occasions such as this one. This window makes me feel like I'm coming home to a warm cottage in the middle of a cornfield, gentle guitars. This window makes me feel very excited, walking outside only wearing a short towel—I walk past a lot of people and I enjoy this. This window makes me feel like life is worth living, which I sure need after having to deal with a bunch of characters like you all year. This window makes me feel like

I'm reading the same story over again, but with an unlikely plot and a disappointing character. This window makes me feel like I'm wearing a vault door. This window makes me feel like Rocky, Number One, and it means I get to drive the fuck away from the house for awhile with the top down and the music blasting. This window makes me feel like I'm never going to get out of that virtual filing cabinet. This window makes me feel like a miniature Billy Graham. This window makes me feel like it's a pretty nice day weather-wise. This window makes me feel like one of those little birds that picks bugs off of water buffalo. This window makes me feel like a winner—it's only noon and I am so proud to have sold 67 shirts already. This window makes me feel much better about taking off from Reagan National Airport. This window makes me feel joyful because I wanted to get the town below and the sky on top and the water for the base. This window makes me feel like I have no sympathy for Milosevic. This window makes me feel really charged—I have it in front of me at my workplace and I feel a positive energy when I look at it everyday. This window makes me feel like I love him like a stray pet off the street, but nonetheless I feel my blood pooling on the ground, and I can feel its crimson liquidity forming around me. This window makes me feel like I must have had a wonderful breakfast; I think it was mainly the fact that it was warm, and it makes me wanna rush home and prepare it again. This window makes me feel good inside and I want to be able to feel this same thing while taking on the challenges of becoming a sergeant. This window makes me feel like I'm the source of the problem and I don't want the two of them to be mean to each other. This window makes me feel angry because even though I don't want to rehash the funding issue in this month's column, I do feel compelled to address the questions and comments I received. This window makes me feel unsafe and vulnerable being dressed in a top which is not tucked into my track-suit bottoms. This window makes me feel like I have the key to exploring myself. This window makes me feel like a mondo dork—I've mostly recovered my dignity from this self-demoralizing view, but, wow, I'm a huge loser. This window makes me feel like I have a deep peace within my soul, but I'm not suggesting that this makes me a better person, or that I look down upon others. This window makes me feel like I want to rob a liquor store just to make ends meet. This window makes me feel all tingly inside like when I was walking on the warm sand and playing in the shiny warm water—I'll be back next summer. This window makes me feel like I could go back home anytime I wanted to. This window makes me feel like I've messed up everything—not only for myself but for my department too. This window makes me feel like something weird is going on because there are a lot of birds swirling around or circling in on something. This window makes me feel like I'm part of the parade even though I'm up here and have to be at my desk. This window makes me feel like I should learn how to burn my own CDs instead of asking my friends to do it for me. This window makes me feel really confused about what people expect from me—I guess I'll know more when I get a response and I can't believe it's almost 5 o'clock and I haven't gotten a response yet. This window makes me feel very badly about the whole Garden Club mix-up. This window makes me feel like I live inside a jackhammer, I can't take it anymore, and it looks like the construction is never going to end. This window makes me feel like it's not my fault if the one I love is into porn—talk about signs focusing on behaviors and observations and reactions to them. This window makes me feel really young again because I'm working on an elk-handled bowie knife from scratch. This window makes me feel really uneasy even though I hate to make performance-based arguments without any code. This window makes me feel so good that I don't mind doing anything that I consider safe, sane, and consensual. This window makes me feel like my own goals and those of the organization are in line when I talk about pay, promotion, and quality of work. This window makes me feel like I'm looking at a plate-sized moth on his back, the sun setting on the Bon Jovi sweatshirts and Princess Diana tees. This window makes me feel so truly international, so cosmopolitan, so weirded out now that we have two Au Bon Pains. This window makes me feel relaxed because I'm working with my dad and enjoying every minute of it and I know he has confidence in me as a horse shoer. This window makes me feel like going to bed. This window makes me feel like I should explain that the photo is way hotter than I am in real life and most days I just wear whatever is on the floor. This window makes me feel disrespected and insignificant because I consider myself to be a serious, hard-working goal-oriented kind of person. This window makes me feel like I can.

Notes:

Why I Do What I do Why He Does What He Does was written as a poetics statement for the N 49 15.832 – W 123 05.921 [POSITION COLLOQUIUM], Vancouver, 2008.

Identity Theft was presented as a talk at San Francisco's *Small Press Traffic* reading series (April, 2005). The italicized sections were written by David Buuck.

1-800 Flowers was written on the occasion of *Zukofsky 100/The Louis Zukofsky Centennial Conference*. I was eager to write a response to Zukofsky's poem *80 Flowers*, in part, because the poem raises complex questions about references and borrowed sources. Part essay and part poem, *1-800-Flowers* uses Zukofsky's own form in 80 Flowers of 8-line stanzas with 5 words per line and no punctuation.

[R E A D I N G] was written in response to an invitation to participate in the Free Biennial Public Art Festival of 2002 (New York). Because the event took place in April, "Poetry Month", I composed a text that foregrounds the "invisible" institutional writing of poetry reading calendars. The complete version of the text exists as a chapbook with housepress (2003).

LIT was written in 2006 on the occasion of Tim Davis' photography exhibit *Illillumination* (Greenberg Van Doren Gallery). Tim invited me to write a text for the catalogue that took into account his thematic interest in "light" for this series of photographs.

National Laureate assembles lines of poetry from each of The United States Poet Laureates.

HI, MY NAME IS is a libretto, commissioned in 2005, by composer John Supko.

A Hemingway Reader was recently published as a No Press chapbook. On the back cover of *The Sun Also Also Rises*, I write: "When I was 13, my brother gave me a copy of Hemingway's *The Sun Also Rises*. It was my first foray into real Literature and I hated it. Even with little or no way to enter the novel, I dutifully slugged through it (I mean, what is cog-nak anyway?) Years later, I have returned to revisit the relationship. In this version, I have erased my way through Hemingway's original text, leaving behind only the phrases that begin with the pronoun I." *My Sun Also Rises* translates the erased version of the first part into my own experience of moving to downtown Manhattan in 1981. In the chapbook version, there is a 3rd book, Also Also Also Rises, The Sun, written by Nayland Blake.

THIS WINDOW MAKES ME FEEL, written in 2002, was propelled by my interest in subjectivity through appropriation. I.e., what would a text read like if it were entirely subjective, but not my personal subjectivity. I started by googling the phrase "this feels" or "this makes me feel." The further I wrote into this text, the more it resonated as a response to 9-11, even though none of the borrowed language speaks directly to that event. A complete version is available online at www.ubu.com.

Roof Books are published by
Segue Foundation • 300 Bowery • New York, NY 10012
Visit our website at **seguefoundation.com**

Roof Books are distributed by
SMALL PRESS DISTRIBUTION
1341 Seventh Avenue • Berkeley, CA. 94710-1403.
Phone orders: 800-869-7553
spdbooks.org

Robert Fitterman is the author of *Metropolis 1-15*, *Metropolis 16-29*, *Metropolis XXX: The Decline and Fall of the Roman Empire*, and, forthcoming, *Sprawl: Metropolis 30A*. Several of his books are collaborations with visual artists, including *war, the musical* with Dirk Rowntree and *The Sun Also Also Rises* with Nayland Blake. He teaches writing and poetry at NYU and in the Bard College, Milton Avery School of Graduate Studies. He lives in NYC with poet Kim Rosenfield and their daughter Coco.

I had a suspicion about this work. I mistrust all frank and simple poetry. This book makes me feel like my trust was wasted. I finally had somebody verify the story. I thought it was accidental. I lost the disgusted feeling and was happy. This book makes me feel like I end up with nothing, but somehow it makes me feel better. I rather liked it. The soft, brushed covering is removable and easy to clean. Adjustable strap holds poems in desired position. New bolder and larger print is easier to see and read. Casing made of 50% post-consumer content. PMA certified nontoxic. Featuring a n outstanding one-of-a-kind circle design, this eye-catching creation is certain to become a topic of conversation.   *—Charles Bernstein*

Rob the Plagiarist is a brilliant investigation of the publics and counterpublics of poetry in our time. No one has a better ear for the mediated languages of our culture in general than the author of this unique book. From the awakening of a mass "Rob" by the impersonal hail of a stranger over the phone *("'Monsieur Langdon?' a man's voice said"),* to a final poem in which an online multitude addresses us through hundreds of anonymous windows, *Rob the Plagiarist* is poetry about the making of collective life—the generation of diverse, politically ambiguous, and often conflicting senses of belonging—through multiple forms of rhetoric, association, and style. This book makes me feel like Rob Fitterman is many Robs, all of them poetic virtuosos.   *—Sianne Ngai*

Jaques le fataliste. Jack the Modernist. From Denis Diderot to Robert Glück, Fitterman carries on a long tradition of fabricated autobiography, genuinely confessional fiction, and full-out appropriation. But as we know from Jack Torrance, who typed an entire manuscript of the one repeated, plagiarized line: all work and no play makes Jack a dull boy. With Fitterman, a plagairist extraordinaire, we have all the play and all the work together in some of the smartest and sharpest textual interventions yet. From a jacquard bathrobe to Jacques Rancière, Jackson Mac Low to a jackhammer, here are the textual hijacks that let you know you've been rob(bed).   *—Craig Dworkin*